AS Media Studies
UNIT 1

AQA

Module 1: Reading the Media

Chris Bruce

Philip Allan Updates
Market Place
Deddington
Oxfordshire
OX15 0SE

Tel: 01869 338652
Fax: 01869 337590
e-mail: sales@philipallan.co.uk
www.philipallan.co.uk

ISBN-13: 978-0-86003-944-0
ISBN-10: 0-86003-944-7

We are grateful to *Maxim* and to the *Yorkshire Post* for allowing us to reproduce material in questions 2 and 4.

This guide has been written specifically to support students preparing for the AQA AS Media Studies Unit 1 examination. The content has been neither approved nor endorsed by AQA and remains the sole responsibility of the authors.

Printed by MPG Books, Bodmin

Environmental information
The paper on which this title is printed is sourced from managed, sustainable forests.

Contents

Introduction

■ ■ ■

Content Guidance

■ ■ ■

Questions and Answers

Introduction

About this guide

This unit guide is for students following the AQA AS Media Studies course. It deals with Unit 1, which examines the content of **Module 1: Reading the Media**. There are three sections to this guide:

- **Introduction** — this provides advice on how to use this guide. It outlines what the unit examines and explains its relationship with the overall AS Media Studies specification. There are suggestions on how to prepare and revise for the exam and key tips on how to succeed in this unit.
- **Content Guidance** — this explains how to approach textual analysis. It outlines a framework that will help you develop your analytical skills and use the Key Concepts, which are central to this unit. This section covers a wide range of concepts that will help you tackle any type of media text.
- **Questions and Answers** — the questions in the exam for this unit are usually very similar, although the range of possible answers is complex and very wide. This section therefore gives sample answers from typical A-grade and C-grade candidates. Each essay is interspersed with examiner comments concerning the Key Concepts and the quality of the response. You will be able to see where marks are allocated and where Assessment Objectives are met.

How to use this guide

The best way to use this guide is to work through it sequentially. After reading the Introduction and the Content Guidance, choose a text and try to write an analysis like those given in the Question and Answer section. To practice writing these kinds of essay, you could write a detailed plan that is not just a set of notes; analyse and evaluate each point, and link them so that the argument flows smoothly from one point to the next. Afterwards, compare your work with the grade-A candidates' responses, paying close attention to the examiner's comments. Reflect on the terminology you omitted or which points you failed to argue logically to their conclusion.

The AS specification

The AS Media Studies course aims to:

- provide you with a conceptual framework that will give you the critical tools necessary to carry out your own readings and investigations, and generate your own questions about the mass media
- enable you to engage with theory, research and ideas relating to the media

- build on, develop and extend your own interests, knowledge and enjoyment of media texts and technologies

In particular, Unit 1 aims to introduce you to the Key Concepts underpinning the specification. You will familiarise yourself with these by applying them to a wide range of media texts.

However, you should be aware that it is not advisable to look at this unit in isolation. Some of the skills that are being assessed also apply to Units 2 and 3.

Examinable skills

The examinable skill being tested in Unit 1 is Assessment Objective (AO) 1 and this is worth 30% of your AS qualification. AO1 asks candidates to show their understanding of a text through the confident and informed application of the Key Concepts. Candidates should evaluate texts and ideas using the Key Concepts. This means that you must produce a textual analysis that employs relevant Key Concepts to reveal what a text is communicating to an audience.

Using the Key Concepts

These are outlined in the Content Guidance section. For this unit, you need to be familiar with the Key Concepts of media language, media representations and media audiences. But don't forget that the other Key Concepts may be relevant too, and you should try not to use them mechanically. For instance, some aspects of media language will be more appropriate than others in illuminating the ideas a particular text is attempting to communicate.

Evaluating texts

As well as discussing the meaning of a particular text in terms of denotation and connotation, you must evaluate the way it works. It is no use stating that 'the lighting in the image is dark and this connotes a depressive atmosphere' unless you attempt to evaluate the text and its signifiers. Why is the lighting like this? What messages are the producers of the text trying to send to the audience by using this type of lighting? Without some form of evaluation you are not covering all aspects of AO1.

Style and making connections

In addition to the above skills, you must be able to:
- write coherently and concisely
- 'think on your feet' by being prepared for any media text that is given to you
- not only show an understanding of the Key Concepts and how to apply them but also show the relationship between them

- use your knowledge of texts similar to the one given to you in the exam in order to try and evaluate it

Study skills and revision strategies

There are many ways to revise and prepare for exams. Some are very personal and you will not be able to follow all of them. The key to success is to be honest with yourself and stick to the revision targets that you set. A good way of familiarising yourself with the exam format is to obtain copies of old papers, perhaps through your teacher. You could also ask your teacher to obtain some past exam scripts from years when students in your centre did well. This will enable you to read effective and successful analyses of the chosen texts.

Better still, you could gather your own examples of appropriate texts — the most suitable ones being those that provide plenty of scope for discussing the Key Concepts.

Below is a suggested revision strategy for Unit 1:
- Organise your learning materials and folders so that you have a section for each of the Key Concepts and for textual analysis practice. Collate the Key Concepts, general concepts and media-specific terminology into a checklist.
- Find out the dates of all your examinations and then plan a revision timetable — you should do this at least 2 months before your exams begin. Make sure there are no clashes in your exam table, and plan sensibly around your busiest period.
- Familiarise yourself with the types of text that may be given to you and the specific requirements of each.
- Make sure you understand the Assessment Objective for this unit. A close under-standing of the Assessment Objective means that you will be confident in the exam because you will know exactly what the examiners are actually examining.
- Make certain that your knowledge of the Key Concepts is thorough. The more elements of each Key Concept that you are aware of, the better you are likely to do.
- Get to know the format and layout of the exam paper by comparing past papers for similarities and differences.
- Read the principal examiner's report on previous exams. This will alert you to the mistakes that students have made in the past and which you need to avoid. If your teacher does not have access to a copy, the report is available on the AQA website at **www.aqa.org.uk**.
- Carefully analyse the register and style of sample essays. Scrutinise the use of terminology and the way that the candidates frame their answers.
- Organise a meeting with other members of your class to discuss issues about the exam. This will also give you a supportive forum to practise analysing some texts.
- In the week of the exam, avoid compromising on sleep. Lack of sleep is likely to make you prone to panic or anxiety.

When you are in the exam, be sure to use your time wisely. Some students find it helpful to break down the available time into sections. A method of doing this is suggested below, but remember that it really depends on the particular text that you are given:

- **Section A** — 5 minutes. Give an overall outline of the key ideas that the text is communicating to its target audience. Analytical detail need only be hinted at during this stage. You could try to explain at least one main point by employing the Key Concepts.
- **Section B** — 45 minutes. This is the main body of your response. Start at the beginning of the text (or the top of the image) and work down. You might pick one important part of the text to focus on.
- **Section C** — 5 minutes. Having analysed the main areas of the text, write an overall evaluation of what it is trying to communicate to its audience and the ideas it is expressing through its mediated representation.
- **Section D** — 5 minutes. Go back over the essay. Read it through for clarity and good English. Finally, for each point that you have discussed, check that you used the three Key Concepts for this unit, and that you therefore have a sophisticated analysis.

The unit test

The Unit 1 examination consists of one question, which asks you to analyse a previously unseen media text or texts. A 'text' is defined as an image or artefact drawn from a wide range of mass media sources; print, moving image or even audio texts may be used. If you are asked to respond to a single text, it may consist of, for example, a front page of a magazine coupled with contents and features pages. The text will have been chosen especially with the Key Concepts in mind; it may be taken from a popular or 'alternative' (non-mainstream) context but will always be chosen so as to allow the Key Concepts to be the main focus of the analysis.

The exam is 75 minutes long, and is worth 30% of your overall AS mark. Of this time, 15 minutes is allocated to a close reading of the text. During this time, candidates are not permitted to start writing their final response, but are allowed to start making short notes on the main points and on how their answer might be structured. The term 'reading' can apply to a still, moving or aural (radio/sound) image. In an exam based on a moving image (television advertisement, film clip, excerpt from a television text, film trailer etc.), the text is normally shown three times, and often the best approach is to avoid making any notes during the first screening. The subsequent screenings are when detailed notes should start to emerge.

Make sure that you read the instructions given on the exam paper and the guidance offered very carefully. This will help focus your answer on the Key Concepts and ensure that you avoid producing an unstructured description of the text.

Content
Guidance

This section gives you all the essential information about the content of Unit 1, takes you through the main points in the specification and outlines the methods and strategies that you might use to do your best in the exam.

It provides guidance on how to employ the Key Concepts for Unit 1 — **language**, **genre**, **audiences** and **representations**. It also outlines others, such as **values and ideology** and **institutions**, which appear elsewhere in the Media Studies course, but are less likely to be needed in Unit 1.

The first part of this section outlines the Key Concepts and shows how you should use them. Some advice on how to make your analyses richer and more comprehensive is also provided. This section then guides you through the process of writing a timed response with a rigorous use of all the appropriate Key Concepts. Finally, there are tips on how to integrate the all-important evaluation with your reading of the text.

Remember that what follows is for guidance only. The exam demands a flexible approach which shows that you can analyse any media text.

You shouldn't, therefore, confine yourself to using only what is covered here. For instance, if you think that there is an important point to make about the ideological connotations of a text, then make it — the point may be crucial to your grade.

The Key Concepts

The Key Concepts constitute the single most important framework for the whole Media Studies course. They have evolved as a means of understanding a text by using a critical framework, rather than just making unconnected and meaningless observations. A scientific evaluation would employ accurate terminology, correctly and methodically applied, to demonstrate that a legitimate procedure had been followed and that the results were valid. Your approach to Media Studies should be equally rigorous. All AS subjects, whether they are arts or sciences, require:

- a reasoned argument that avoids a solely subjective viewpoint
- the use of a structured intellectual framework
- an evaluation that demonstrates to teachers, examiners and fellow students that the analysis has been properly conducted

What follows is a brief overview of the Key Concepts and how you might think about using them, not only in Unit 1 but in all your subsequent Media Studies work. For Unit 1, the emphasis is on media language, genre, media audiences and media representations. It is important to stress, however, that you should not see the Key Concepts as being discrete and separate. In fact, with repeated attempts to perfect the style and structure of a Unit 1 response, you will see that they work in unison with each other.

The mnemonic 'RAILING' might help you remember the Key Concepts in an exam situation. It stands for:

- **R**epresentations
- **A**udiences
- **I**nstitutions
- **L**anguage
- **I**deology
- **N**arrative
- **G**enre

Language

This is one of the most important of the Key Concepts and it is probably the one that you will use the most. It asks you to consider **visual elements**, such as lighting, mastheads, dress codes and headlines, as well as **aural codes**, such as the use or type of music and sound effects.

Reference to media language should usually be made early on in Unit 1 analyses. If you are discussing a visual text, for example, you might mention that the lighting is 'high-key' and that this leads to a sense of joy or happiness within the image (as long as the other signifiers support such a statement).

Also, consider the **narrative structure** of the media piece that you are analysing. It may be a poster or an advert, but it will still imply a narrative 'moment'. What has happened before it? What may happen after we (the audience) are gone? Are there enigmas or mysteries within the image? Are there codes of action? Is something bad going to happen? Are binary opposites set up — a contrast or contradiction that makes the text arresting and draws the audience in?

Genre

Genre is the type or category into which a text can be placed. However, you should be aware that some texts may fit into more than one category. A lot of complicated genre theory has been written so you are not expected to know it all. The expectation at AS is that you recognise key features of texts, their variations, what their effect might be on an audience, and how genre helps audiences feel comfortable and understand the meaning of a text. A framework that might help you define a genre is the acronym **NICS**. The letters stand for **narrative**, **iconography**, **characters** and **settings**. A genre will have typical aspects of these.

Certain signifiers are key identifiers of genre. For example, tumbleweed rolling across a desert plain often implies a text from the Western genre. A character such as a sheriff would also be an indicator, especially if he was standing outside a saloon. The type of text would therefore be confirmed through the setting.

A **postmodern** text will probably be made up of several genres. For instance, postmodern rap music features 'sampling' of classical music. A text might be **intertextual**, which means it makes reference to a previous image, text or genre. For example, Lloyds Bank and Red Bull ran adverts that closely shadowed a fairy story. Alternatively, texts might parody an existing text. Recognising the mimicking of key characteristics from a previous text makes audiences feel powerful and culturally informed. *Scary Movie* parodies the conventions of teen-horror films, for example.

Audiences

All texts are made for an audience. Media corporations and companies use texts as opportunities to make profits and promote their products and services. Research is done into audiences to make sure that the media producers are targeting them effectively. Two models for analysing audience are **segmentation** methods and the **socio-economic scale**.

The segmentation approach considers audiences not as massed millions but in terms of individuals and subgroups. For instance, the 15 million viewers of *EastEnders* will include a wide range of people, differentiated from each other by gender, age, professional status, geographical location, religion, ethnicity and so on. Seeing audiences in these terms will help you to measure the feelings, reactions and aspirations of a mass audience and to identify which signifiers in a particular text communicate directly with each of these subgroups.

Another popular model is the socio-economic scale which groups media receivers into six categories based on professional status and spending power: A, B, C1, C2, D and E. Group E consists of those who have the lowest disposable income, such as people who draw benefits, OAPs and students. Group A comprises people with very high earning potential and a correspondingly large budget for spending, for example hospital consultants or managing directors. Attached to the socio-economic scale are notions of 'taste' and certain expectations about types of consumption. Members of group A would not be expected to eat at McDonald's, for example. In terms of media consumption, people in the top group might gravitate towards high-culture texts such as those most often seen on BBC2 or heard on Radio 4.

This model was originally conceived to allow media producers to target their texts at appropriate demographics, but defining people by their income can lead to sweeping assumptions about each group. It would be wise to use other analytical audience models alongside this one when looking at a text in the Unit 1 exam.

Another important factor to consider is **audience positioning**. When constructing media texts, producers think long and hard about the feelings and emotional reactions that they want to elicit from the audience. Whether you see this as manipulative or as a clever organisation of material, it is your job to analyse and evaluate how producers achieve the reactions they want.

Every text has a mode of address and creates a point of view. In a charity advertisement, the technical choices will have been made in order to provoke sympathetic reactions. For example, the camera may be looking down on a malnourished child from a high angle and via a long shot which shows the child as small and isolated. In this case, the audience has been positioned by the text's producer to receive the text in an emotional way.

Representations

Texts are carriers of information and confirmation that apparently tell us about the world: how people dress, how they think, what they say etc. As an audience, we receive these signals and often passively accept that the text is telling the truth. But is it? It is your job to unpick the text and evaluate whether it offers a just and exact representation of what is actually going on in our culture or the wider world.

A useful acronym for the key points in this concept is **PPE**. Representation is concerned with how media texts present and mediate ideas about:
* **people**. How are they represented? What activities are they doing? Are men represented as active and women as passive?

- **places**. Are certain aspects of a place shown/heard over others?
- **events**. In the represented event, what is included and what is left out? Why do you think that this is?

The theorist Richard Dyer suggests four areas to consider when analysing representation:
- representations of the world and how the technical language of media images helps describe that world
- the way in which 'types' (especially stereotypes) are used to stand in for whole social groups
- the particular media institution, and the personnel in that institution who make the decisions that influence representations
- what the audience believes is being represented, which might include readings not anticipated by the producers of the text

You should also think about the **language** a text employs. Is it gender-specific? Does it favour one gender over another? Consider whether the text uses stereotypes and, if so, whether they have a damaging or positive effect. For example, in an advertising image a woman might be heavily made-up and wearing clothing that emphasises her body; this image could be seen as empowering, because the woman holds the attention of men, but it could also be interpreted as patriarchal, because she is subjected to the male gaze.

Social class is another important aspect of representation. Decide what kind of lifestyle the text is promoting and whether it evokes an aspirational response (wanting to emulate the lifestyle) or a transactional response (recognising the attractions of the lifestyle but not seeing how it would benefit you personally). In dealing with class, however, be careful not to make clumsy assumptions. The divisions between classes are blurred and you should always base your reading of a text on the signifiers in it. Consider material objects such as clothing, cars, interior décor and so on, and take account of characters' professions and their speech, accent and use of vocabulary. These will give indications as to affluence, position and, perhaps, class status.

Finally, pay attention to the processes of how representation can be communicated. Representations are almost certainly influenced by the technical decisions that shape a text's construction. For example, the representation of a fictional character or real-life person in a text will be affected if they are photographed:
- in reduced light, which implies a depressing emotional tone
- from a high angle, which looks down on them
- in a dark costume, which represents the character's solemness
- in restrictive clothing, such as a blouse with a high button, which gives the wearer an appearance of being constrained

These are simple examples but they show that representations are affected by technical decisions, which are often made with the intention of subtly positioning the audience so as to provoke the desired dominant reading. You should refer to pages 20–21 for a more detailed analysis.

Values and ideology

Representations and ideology are very closely linked. If you look at some of the explanations above, you will find many areas where they overlap; try to think of them as flowing on from one another organically.

Ideology is a complex area. It deals with how messages, values, morals and beliefs are evident in texts. Unfortunately, these signifiers are almost invisible. You need to look for clues that lead you to identify ideological trends. This becomes problematic because ideologies are not necessarily consciously put there by the producer of the text, but often enter subconsciously, arising from an assumption that what they are representing is normal and beyond question. This often applies to ideologies around gender (e.g. how women and men should behave), which tend to get perpetuated when certain styles and types of text are repeated by numerous producers. One factor that might explain why women historically have been represented as subservient to men is that often men have been controllers of media networks and decision-makers. With the recent rise of more women to positions of power within the media, there has been an increasing tendency to represent women as active, intelligent individuals outside the home.

Use the following framework to help you to think more clearly about conducting an ideological analysis. Use the six terms as starting points for questioning the representation of normality in your text.
- **Patriarchal**. Does the text suggest that it is normal for men to be more powerful than women?
- **Heterosexual**. Does the text suggest that being heterosexual is more acceptable than being gay or bisexual? Are there any homosexual representations at all?
- **Bourgeois**. Does the text represent middle-class values about the home, family and morality as the norm? For instance, it could suggest that everybody should be aspiring to own their own home.
- **Familial**. Does the text show the nuclear family unit (a man, a woman and children) as normal? Does it exclude one-parent families or single-parent providers?
- **Capitalist**. Does the text suggest that aspiring to acquire money and material wealth is the norm? This may be represented through the image of a fast car parked on the drive outside the house, for example.
- **Nationalism**. Does the text give one particular nation or culture greater importance than another? One way of analysing this is to consider whether certain ethnic groups are absent from, or poorly portrayed in, the text.

Institutions

Institutions comprise media businesses, their practices (ways of doing things) and their organisations. Studying institutions means looking at how these factors affect texts in terms of content, form and issues of inclusion and exclusion.

A good example of this is soap operas. BBC1's *EastEnders* is considered to be a 'gritty' and hard-hitting prime-time serial, tackling issues that have often been passed over by other television companies. This might be because the BBC is a public service broadcaster, unlike ITV, which is commercially funded. Some argue that ITV's *Coronation Street* is a 'softer' soap opera, which avoids difficult issues such as rape and homosexuality, for fear of deterring advertisers. Decisions taken by management personnel therefore influence the nature of the text itself.

An insight into how institutions determine the shape and content of texts lies in soap operas' handling of the issue of teenage pregnancy. Again, it is argued that the portrayal in *EastEnders* of Sonia Jackson's experiences dealt with the trauma and moral questions directly, while *Coronation Street*'s story about Sarah Louise Platt showed fewer of the hardships involved. Some criticised it for inviting young girls to see too many positive aspects to being a teenage mother.

It is impossible to know everything about the media institution that produced the text you are studying — especially in the case of an unseen text in the Unit 1 exam. Don't let this overwhelm you; instead, concentrate on investigating the types of text that particular institutions create. The table below will help you do this:

Institution	Type of text produced
Radio and television	
Public service	• Public service broadcast remit • Serving minority and niche audiences • Not necessarily driven by ratings or play lists • Commercial recognition important but not vital
Commercial	• Some public service purpose but mainly driven by ratings and profit • Mainstream, low-risk output • Programmes often structured around advertising slots • Sponsorship, product placement etc. central to output
Newspapers	
Red-top tabloids	• Usually celebrity-based • Sensationalise trivial events • Reflect popular opinion and accused of creating moral panics • Often simplify events or omit complex political or economic stories
Blue-top tabloids	• More sophisticated audience than red-top tabloids • Often right wing, and therefore highly protective of marriage, heterosexuality, national identity etc. • Headlines (as for red-top tabloids) are often dramatic and exaggerated through alliteration, rhyme or puns
Broadsheets	• Explore political and economic news in more detail than the tabloids, with greater space in which to do this • News and entertainment values are often 'high-culture' • Advertisements placed in these papers reflect higher aspirations than those placed in tabloids

Institution	Type of text produced
Film	
Mainstream	• Cause-and-effect narrative, using montage, in language that will not confuse a general audience • Usually structured around recognisable narratives and characters that don't challenge the genre • Often involve high production values and large budgets • Stars are associated with the product and often bring a 'brand' identity with them
Alternative	• Target niche or marginalised audiences • Narratives might be constructed differently from mainstream films • Genres can be redefined • Usually associated with art-house or progressive styles • Often made on a not-for-profit basis

In practice, many of these features overlap. A text may have both a public service and a commercial context, or alternative elements could be found within a mainstream production.

The concept of institutions is closely connected to representations and ideology, and knowing this may help you to structure your response in the exam. You might make an analysis of how a particular character is represented, in what way the position or inclusion of this character contributes to a particular ideology, and finally how this aspect of the text hints at some of the values and attitudes of the institution that produced it.

You should also familiarise yourself with some of the concepts involved in institutions. This will mean making notes on terms such as film star, scheduling, financing, competition, shareholders, media laws, issues of morality, news values, news sources, Office for Communications (OFFCOM), playlists and sponsorship.

Analytical frameworks

Selby and Cowdery's concepts of analysis

In their book *How to Study Television* (2nd edn, Palgrave Macmillan, 1995), Keith Selby and Ron Cowdery offer a comprehensive framework for analysing texts. This uses media terminology and is methodical in its approach; if you employ this analytical model, therefore, you will be in a good position to read a text fully and successfully.

Below is a slightly amended version of their methods. Although the framework originated from a study of television and the moving image, it can also be applied to still images and, in part, to radio or sound texts.

Technical and *mise-en-scène* codes

Selby and Cowdery split the analytical tools needed for deconstructing a text into two groups:

- **technical** codes
- *mise-en-scène* codes

These groups should be seen not as separate but as complementary to one another. The first group focuses on the technical aspects of textual construction, while the second group, meaning 'putting the scene together', directs readers' attention to visual signifiers in the image. These codes are listed in the following table:

Technical codes	Mise-en-scène codes
• Shot size • Camera angle • Lenses • Composition • Focus • Lighting • Film stock • Film colour, e.g. black and white/Technicolor • Sound/music/sound effects* • Colour, e.g. golden = warm*	• Setting • Props • NVC (non-verbal communication) • Dress
*These two technical codes are not included in Selby and Cowdery's book and have been added by the author of this guide.	

Connotations

A **denotation** describes what an image actually shows, while a **connotation** gives its deeper meaning. A range of possible connotations for each code is given below to help you see how to apply this model in practice.

Technical codes

Denotation	Connotation
Shot size — e.g. long shot	A character shot from far away seems removed from the audience, distanced, isolated or alone
Camera angle — e.g. low-angle shot	A low down shot, looking up at the subject, implies that it is more important than the audience
Lenses — e.g. telephoto lens	Selecting and focusing on one object or subject gives it exclusive importance
Composition — e.g. symmetrical framing	This implies that the filmed space has order and that the inhabitants of that space are organised and tidy

Denotation	Connotation
Focus — e.g. blur	In a still image (e.g. in an advert), a blurred background and a focused image of a car imply speed
Lighting — e.g. low-key state	The lighting implies a sombre feeling without the need for speech
Film stock — e.g. grainy/speckled/under-exposed	This gives a documentary or 'realist' effect
Film colour — e.g. Technicolor, overall finish	If the colour of a film is unusually bright, it has a fantasy feel; if a film's finish is 'murky' or grey, it has connotations of dullness
Sound/music/sound effects — e.g. 'grave' (solemn) music	The soundtrack emphasises a solemn feeling
Colour — e.g. character wearing white	White has connotations of purity and innocence, implying that the character shares these

Mise-en-scène codes

Denotation	Connotation
Setting — e.g. affluent, well-decorated, middle-class home with a number of hi-tech gadgets and in an urban environment	The inhabitants are successful and probably young; they have an interest in technology and know how it works; they take pride in their living space and use it to signify their wealth, fortune and taste
Props — e.g. a muddy bike in a house	The character is indifferent to getting dirty; he or she enjoys open spaces and likes the environment; he or she is not concerned about the dirty bike being inside the house
NVC — e.g. hunched shoulders, head hanging down	The character is feeling vulnerable, unhappy or depressed
Dress — e.g. a young character wears a brown, chunky cardigan	The character rejects fashion in favour of comfort (and perhaps security); brown is a warm colour and is connected to Earth and nature

This approach should give you additional confidence when tackling your Unit 1 essay. Use the Selby and Cowdery model to support your own analysis and evaluation of the text you are studying.

Now that we have discussed the analytical frameworks you need, the next stage is to discuss how to organise the exam essay so that your investigative evidence can be put to best use and secure you a high grade.

Applying the frameworks

Analysing your text

Although it is important to apply critical frameworks to the study of media texts, the danger of doing so is that you can end up producing a mechanical response, employing the models of analysis so rigidly that your essay sounds as if it has been written by a computer. For instance:

> The woman wears a red dress. Therefore she is sexually charged and passionate. She lives in a high-rise flat so she must be poor. There is a bottle of wine on the table so she must like to drink alcohol.

This is far too simplistic. What if the red dress is one she wears for work? In any case, it doesn't necessarily follow that she is feeling 'sexy' at this moment. Nor does the flat actually have to be hers. Try to think clearly and logically and use your experience to develop your analysis beyond superficial comments.

The following is a better analysis (though there may be other ways to respond to the same material):

> The woman wears a red dress. This colour could connote passion and lust, but her non-verbal communication seems to suggest otherwise. She appears tired, perhaps having just come home from work. The bottle of wine and a single glass that sit on the table connote that she leads a hectic life and may find some comfort in relaxing with a drink after work. Overall, the image, which looks like an attempt to capture a realistic moment, has a documentary feel to it and could perhaps be commenting on the damaging nature of twenty-first-century lifestyles.

Evaluating your analysis

It is vital that you assess what you have analysed. Here is another example of a strait-jacketed 'list' of denotation and connotation:

> The man in the image has a pinstriped suit on. Therefore he must be a business man. The house featured in the text is large. This must mean that the people are rich. The children smile. This means that they are happy.

This response is one-dimensional and lacks depth. You should always use the evidence given and then reflect on it after each point. Survey what you have said and make an evaluation:

> The house featured is very large and it is clear that the institution which produced this image wants to signify that their target audience either shares this lifestyle or aspires to do so. It is possibly targeting socio-economic groups A–C1, which have a large disposable income. The references in the copy quoting the people who are interviewed suggest that their interest in green issues would make them 'societally conscious' achievers — they are successful, but spiritually aware and environmentally careful. It definitely promotes a particular lifestyle and follows a typical trend witnessed in texts from the same genre.

This second version is much more mature in style and attempts to distance itself from the image and make an evaluation of what the signifiers might collectively be communicating.

Evaluating denotations and connotations signals a much more intellectual analysis. You should also demonstrate the context of the text by relating it briefly to other relevant texts that you have encountered. Don't see the exam text in isolation. Texts chosen for the exam may well have intertextual references and examiners will expect you to comment on these to show that you have studied a wide range of media.

Critical autonomy

Being critically autonomous means having the ability to write your own views and interpretations instead of rehearsing an analysis learned from your teacher. This is a difficult skill to master, but it will gain you higher marks.

We are all the subjects of **socialisation**; our different experiences and interactions make us what we are. This means that one person's reaction to a text will be different from another's. There are a number of common assumptions about any text that are shared by our culture and society. For instance, a character wearing black may suggest death, mourning, a 'dark' person, evil and so on. But examiners will also be interested in your personal readings of a text, so long as it is based on the Key Concepts.

It is tempting to try to guess the examiner's agenda and assume that there is a single 'correct' reading of a text, or an ultimate answer. There will be central themes and focus points in a text, but the Unit 1 mark scheme states that 'Most students will stick to expected areas, but if the unexpected and unpredictable is backed up with reference to the text then…(if it is apt and focused)…it should be marked positively. Thus the mark scheme is only a guide…'

Writing your exam essay

Structure

There are a number of points to bear in mind when writing a response in this exam. Many students panic and become confused because there are so many points to make, and seemingly all at once. Avoid a single Key Concept approach, and instead analyse by 'clustering' the Key Concepts. For example, analyse the specific part of the text you have chosen with media language. Perhaps then find a connection to its methods of representation, which may lead on to a discussion and analysis of the concept of media audiences. At appropriate points, and certainly at the end of each paragraph, you should make an evaluation to sum up the evidence that you have presented. The strategies that follow will help you structure and sequence your essay.

Concept maps

First, find a focus point in the text you are studying. It might be a central character, a prop or any signifier of colour, costume, setting and so on. Take, for instance, the cover of a teenage-girls' magazine such as *Just Seventeen*. To tackle the main image, make a diagram like the one below, using the three most relevant Key Concepts as headings:

Media language

- **Faces camera = dominant and 'sassy'**
- Fills whole page = emphasis and importance
- Open-mouthed smile = happy and confident

Representations

- All girls should look like this
- Construct the target audience
- Shows constructed beauty as if it is natural
- Girls as objects of sexual desire
- Red signifies passion and sex
- **Constructs codes of behaviour and targets readers who need guidance in this area**

Audience

- C1, C2 and aspirational Ds
- Bright, bouncy and go-getting
- Attractive and appealing
- Gives girls what they 'lack'
- **Signifies what is 'expected' by its audience in terms of how to look/behave**
- Uses and gratifications theory
- Dyer's 'entertainment and utopia' theory

The next stage is to look at the ways in which you can link points together in the different boxes. The three emboldened points in the diagram could be connected together, and it is this skill that the examiners will be looking for: fluent analysis that seamlessly connects one Key Concept to another via a 'focus' area — in this case, the central image. A good way to start your response is by describing — briefly — some of the elements of the image (but only the ones that you are going to make a point about), offering sensible and logical connotations of the denotations given. Below is a paragraph for the diagram that follows this approach:

> The young girl faces the camera, looking directly at the audience, with an open-mouthed smile, perfect teeth and red lips. Her casual stance and position signify that she is confident and in control [media language]. This text clearly appeals to an audience in their mid to late teens but also targets a much younger audience subsection: those who aspire to rise into this group. The 'sassiness' signified by the girl suggests direction for younger

aspirational groups in the audience, clearly offering a construction of how a female should be. The clothing and appearance would appeal to a C1 or C2 audience but with an aspirational D group also being targeted. The absence of ethnic minorities suggests that the magazine's audience is ethnocentrically white and middle class. The text 'naturalises' notions of constructed beauty, class and appearance and signifies a set of values that suggest this to be the norm within this group [representations and audiences].

This flow of concepts — media language leading to representations and audiences — is crucial to a good analysis.

Four Key Concepts which often (though not always) go well in a sequence are:

media language $\longrightarrow$ **representations** $\longrightarrow$ **ideology** $\longrightarrow$ **audiences**

In this instance, your approach could follow these stages:
(1) Describe the key signifiers.
(2) Evaluate how these signifiers represent people, places or events.
(3) Explain how this promotes a set of ideological messages and values that the text (and ultimately the institution) wants you to perceive as the norm. (You might, for higher marks, add a point about why this is so.)
(4) Using the evidence you have written, say who is being targeted and how the text might appeal to this audience. You would need to say whether the audience is fairly represented and communicated with or whether the audience is constructed by the text for the purpose of promoting certain messages and values.

Your own judgement will tell you that certain Key Concepts are more relevant than others to a particular text (e.g. narrative theory was inappropriate for analysing a text from *Ministry of Sound* magazine in the summer 2002 Unit 1 exam). Approach the text in a holistic way — don't, like some past candidates, divide the 60 minutes' writing time into equal-length portions for the four main Key Concepts. You are allowed to section your essay by using separate headings (often the Key Concepts) but there is a danger that you will only discuss that particular Key Concept and avoid relating it to others. Remember that finding connections makes for a much more thorough analysis.

Similarly, some candidates have made the mistake of spending 30 minutes describing signifiers in the text in the first half of their answer and then using the second half to deal with the connotations and evaluations of the points made. It is better to link denotations with their connotations and then evaluate them immediately using the Key Concepts. By producing an essay plan and/or a concept map in the 15 minutes' reading time you will avoid aimless commentary and observation, and will be able to address the analysis itself immediately.

Preparation

It cannot be stated strongly enough that you should analyse a wide range of print, aural and visual texts from outside your cultural experience. This way, you will learn how to look at something about which you have little or no prior knowledge, so that you have to apply the Key Concepts to unearth the meanings behind the text. Students often fall into the trap of being so familiar with a text they forget to analyse it, and instead make bland, unstructured statements which don't employ the critical and conceptual framework.

You should also bear in mind that studying a wide range of texts means becoming familiar with the codes, conventions and key terminology of different media forms — for example, the main terms (e.g. masthead) needed to discuss the front page of a magazine or newspaper. As the brief for the Unit 1 exam suggests, you will need to be knowledgeable about moving-image texts as well (this should be covered in your Unit 2 lessons if you study Film and Broadcast Fiction). Can you name key ingredients of documentary practice if your teacher decides that you will not formally study documentary in Unit 2? It is up to you to study independently — with guidance from your teacher — these unfamiliar forms and genres.

Studying a wide range of texts is also vital to help you avoid analysing a text in isolation. You must attempt to show how its ideas and content seem either similar to or different from other texts from a similar background. For example, a text may have been chosen that gives candidates the opportunity to comment on how it compares with a group of similar texts that have the same representations of young people.

However, you should not use the exam as an opportunity to list everything you have learnt. After learning and practising a range of analytical tools (e.g. Propp's narrative functions or the 'hypodermic needle' theory of audience) it is tempting to use them in your analysis, whether they are relevant or not. You should not approach the text with a set of preconceived ideas, but come to it openly; you will not be rewarded for reciting all you know about Bourdieu's cultural competence theory if it is not relevant to the text being scrutinised.

Different types of text

The specification expects you to have studied a range of texts in preparation for the exam. It is therefore vital that you research independently any types of text that you don't study in class. The types of text are:
- printed
- moving image
- aural (radio)

In addition to the frameworks outlined above, you may need to employ concepts specific to each kind of text. You are also expected to be familiar with some media-specific terminology and to apply it selectively and appropriately in your analysis.

Printed texts

This section addresses chiefly newspapers and magazines. The skills/concepts discussed below still apply to print advertising, but you should also consider the following:

- Is the text for public relations purposes?
- Is it a form of subtle or covert marketing?
- Why does the producer want to promote the product or service in this way?

You should also analyse and evaluate the use and function of language in slogans, tag-lines and so on.

Terminology

Look at the diagram below and the table overleaf. They use a newspaper's front page to introduce some of the terminology involved in understanding how printed texts work.

(1) **Masthead**	This is the name or title of the newspaper; it is usually larger than the rest of the text, and differs in size and layout from the headline; it may be in a box and coloured
(2) **Earpiece**	This is a small advertisement/promotion/offer placed in a corner alongside the masthead
(3) **Date**	The reference point of every newspaper is the date; this is an indication to the reader of when the news actually happened
(4) **Price**	This is important to a potential buyer; prices have been a source of tension between rival titles as they battle for sales
(5) **Headline**	This is a short, snappy and memorable phrase that sums up the story; the font size should be larger than the main copy; the headline is very important on the front page, as this is what attracts the reader
(6) **Byline**	This tells the reader who the article is written by, sometimes followed by their job title
(7) **Photograph**	This often accompanies articles to give the reader visual reference to what is going on in the story
(8) **Caption**	This is a phrase or sentence which 'explains' the photograph; it defines the meaning of the action in the photo itself
(9) **Columns**	This is the typical style of newspaper layout; the copy is arranged in vertical columns
(10) **Print**	In main articles, the print design has the first paragraph in bold, with the first one or two words in capital letters (this is predominant in red- and blue-top tabloids)
(11) **Copy**	The main body of the text
(12) **Banner**	A 'strip' to tell the reader the contents inside; it appears at the top or bottom of the page
(13) **Brief**	A few lines summarising articles that appear later on in the newspaper

Knowing these terms will help make your analysis clear. Some students call the masthead a headline and then get confused when they come to talk about the headline itself. The responses to questions 2 and 4 in the Question and Answer section later in this guide will show you how this terminology is applied.

News values and ideology

The editorial page of a newspaper will reveal the kinds of issues the editor thinks are important. You will need to know something about party politics in order to identify the political positions the various newspapers take. Decide whether a particular newspaper is 'right wing' — a term meaning that, broadly, it advocates a free-market economy, limited reliance on the state benefit and welfare system, and traditional ideas of nuclear families. A left-wing newspaper would, in simple terms, reveal a belief in socialism, with value placed on the NHS, the welfare state, comprehensive education and, traditionally, the nationalisation of key industries and infrastructures such as the railways.

Audiences and institutions

It is also useful to think about other parts of a printed text's contents and features pages. The contents page reveals a good deal about the audience and the institution, indicating what the audience seems to want to consume, but also the choice of subject matter made by the producers, who often 'guide' readers to feel that this is what they should wish to read. In other words, the text constructs the audience by addressing some particular groups and excluding others.

It may be helpful to have an idea of the sales and circulation figures of the main national newspapers. These statistics can be found in the *Media Guardian*, which is available on Mondays. This may give you some extra information about types of audience. Also, you could contact your local newspaper to research its target readership and advertising, and how a local 'voice' is constructed.

Language

You should consider the types of language used in printed texts, and transfer this skill to moving-image media too. Analyse the mode of address to work out how a text is attracting its audience. Does it use:
- slang, colloquial language and/or a rhetorical question?
- an intellectual register (perhaps scientific language in a car advert)?
- techniques such as alliteration, assonance or rhyme?
- borrowed phrases, words or sayings from other texts or within our wider culture, which show elements of intertextuality?

Now evaluate why these techniques have been used. Perhaps the producers of the text want to make their audiences feel special or 'clever' for recognising intertextual features. They might want to engage the audience through a puzzle or an enigma, drawing them in through curiosity. It is important to take some time to study language so that you are prepared to deal with it in an informed way.

Moving-image texts

Many of the concepts required to analyse moving-image texts have been discussed earlier in the guide, but there are a few specific points that you might consider.

Language

Think about film language and how it communicates ideas. The transition techniques of cut, fade and dissolve all have slightly different effects on the film's narrative in terms of how they move filmic space and time forward. A dissolve, for example, is often used to take the audience into a flashback. Consider why the producer of a text has used this device and try to evaluate what it might add to the narrative, characters and themes of a film, or to the product or service in the case of an advert.

Another feature to consider is the 'speed' of the editing across a sequence. The producers of a text might use rapid editing to make the text seem energetic or dynamic. If the editing is spaced out, you should analyse the effect this might have on the characters, objects or products in the sequence.

It might also be worth looking at the cinematography of the text. How does the camera move? Is it fluid, moving freely as it sweeps about the frame? Is the camera static, as if the producers wanted to give a calm effect to the sequence? Analyse these techniques and then evaluate them.

Another key area to focus on is music and sound effects. These are often crucial in emphasising significant aspects of the text. Ask yourself the following:

- What style/genre of music is used? Why?
- What is the music suggesting about the visual image presented to you?
- Which period or decade does it come from? Is this significant?
- Does it complement the visual images or does it have a more contradictory function, perhaps as an ironic comment or as an attempt to undermine the image?

Listen to the lyrics and decide if they are emphatic (meant to underline or emphasise) or symbolic, ironic or contradictory. It is an absolute certainty that a song or a piece of music will have been chosen for a reason and you should comment on this in your analysis and evaluation.

To help you do this you should learn a few musical terms such as grave (solemn) and adagio (slow). These describe the pace and emotional mood of music.

Ideology

Look at how the camera is positioned in relation to the characters in the film or television text. If the audience is given a 'privileged' viewpoint, how does this affect the way that ideologies are presented to us? Consider how features such as the composition of the frame and the lighting guide us subtly towards certain decisions about issues of gender, sexuality or nation.

Institutions

If a text contains 'stars', you should consider the kind of persona that the media, in conjunction with the marketing department of the film studio or television company, have created.

Think about the issues involved in scheduling or transmitting a television text. Is it broadcast during prime time or after the watershed? Does this make a difference to audiences or to representations of people, places and events contained in the text?

If a film has a certificate, you should decide how this affects the way that the audience receives the text.

Aural (radio) texts

To date, no Unit 1 exam text has ever been a sound or aural one, but the specification does allow for this, so you should acquaint yourself with some of the specifics of sound or radio production. Use the table below to help you do so, and refer to question 5 in the Question and Answer section to see these terms in use.

Airtime	This is access to the broadcast airwaves; radio stations can sell their airtime to advertisers
Anchor	Person in a studio who links up with and maintains contact with outside correspondents, interviewees etc.
Bed/pad	Music that a presenter talks over
Bulletin	A summary of the news
Copy	Written material, e.g. a script
DAB	Digital audio broadcasting
Dead air	This is silence, and is usually unintentional
House style	The style of speaking, output and delivery adopted and imposed by a particular radio station
Ident	A short, frequent jingle or stab that identifies a station or programme to listeners
Incue	The words spoken by a presenter to introduce a correspondent or an interviewee
Jingle	A short advert for a programme, presenter or an event
Mix	Combining separate sound sources
News values	These are the 12 factors identified by Galtung and Ruge (1965) as governing the news agenda: frequency; threshold; unambiguity; meaningfulness; consonance; unexpectedness; continuity; composition; cultural proximity; elite persons; personalisation; negativity
OB	Outside broadcasts
Outcue	The words with which a correspondent hands back to the studio
Playlist	A list of records chosen by a radio station for playing
Promise of performance	Radio stations have to inform the Radio Authority of the style and format of their output, and then abide by this promise; therefore, any promises to broadcast certain types of music, regular news, travel updates and so on must be kept

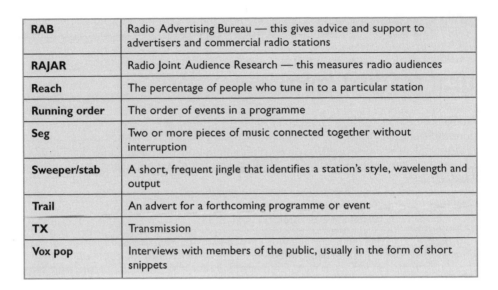

RAB	Radio Advertising Bureau — this gives advice and support to advertisers and commercial radio stations
RAJAR	Radio Joint Audience Research — this measures radio audiences
Reach	The percentage of people who tune in to a particular station
Running order	The order of events in a programme
Seg	Two or more pieces of music connected together without interruption
Sweeper/stab	A short, frequent jingle that identifies a station's style, wavelength and output
Trail	An advert for a forthcoming programme or event
TX	Transmission
Vox pop	Interviews with members of the public, usually in the form of short snippets

Language

Think about the accent of the radio voice, the language used, and the lifestyles and products being promoted through the content and the voices. Decide if the pace of delivery of the sounds connotes speed and dynamism, and the kinds of message this might send an audience in terms of its lifestyle and behaviour.

If the sequence that you are given contains adverts, then what kind of voice-over does it use? Does it feature a famous actor? If so, why was he or she chosen? Is it for being known for a particular skill or style that associates him or her with the product? For example, the presenters Ant and Dec's association with youth-orientated TV secured them the voice-over of an energetic advert for a drink targeted at teenagers.

Genre

From the clues in the text, decide if it is from a commercial radio station, a public-service station or a local/community station (i.e. caters for minority audiences). Is it solely a music station or does its content hint at another function? If it is primarily music based, what type of music is being played? If there are guests, do they have a particular way of attracting an audience?

You should also familiarise yourself with radio drama. Although some see it as inaccessible to young audiences, radio drama is rewarding to analyse, because it uses a set of highly organised sound signifiers to communicate its ideas. All radio drama (and, for that matter, all radio advertising) is recorded in a studio, and therefore all the sounds have to be created. This gives you the opportunity to unravel how a story is told. For instance, if you hear the sound of crickets chirping before you hear any voices, you can guess that the text is probably located on a hot day in the countryside.

Institutions

Think about the differences in output and audience between a public-service and a commercial broadcaster. Perhaps they have different ideas about the function of radio. Is the commercial station aiming to reach a wide audience, or is there evidence to suggest that it provides niche programmes? Identify whether a music station is likely to have a playlist (a favoured list of tracks played regularly throughout transmission). Which do you think are the station's main competitors, and are there marketing activities in the exam extract that could give clues as to how the station promotes itself?

Audience

Look out for clues as to the type of audience being targeted. If the extract includes news bulletins, is the news given briefly, or in depth? What kind of news is included? It could be 'infotainment', or tackle serious topics. Is there a vox pop (interviews with the general public)? What kind of voices are heard? Are they a true sample?

Questions
&
Answers

This section of the guide provides questions and candidate responses typical of the AQA Unit 1 examination. Each question is followed by a grade-A and a grade-C response. The aim is to show what distinguishes a merely competent answer from an excellent one that employs the Key Concepts usefully and thoroughly.

The grade-A examples are not 'model answers'; they do not represent the only, or even necessarily the best, way of answering the question. As you read through them you may think of other points that are equally relevant. Remember that there are numerous ways of approaching any text, and that different texts will produce unique readings by different individuals.

The responses are intended to give you a sense of the essay style that examiners are looking for. Look carefully at the language used, how the terminology is employed and how points are argued. The grade-A answers demonstrate how to combine Key Concepts with critical evaluations, as well as using the material clearly and analysing in a sequential and organised way. The grade-C candidates approach the task in the correct way, but their expression is sometimes awkward and they fail to argue their points convincingly, demonstrating hesitation, a lack of clarity or an inability to utilise the Key Concepts fully.

Examiner's comments

The candidate answers are interspersed with examiner's comments, preceded by the icon *e*. These indicate where credit is due and, in the case of the grade-A answers, show what it is that enables the candidates to score so highly. Particular attention is given to the candidates' use of the examinable skills: knowledge and application of Key Concepts, textual analysis and evaluation. For the grade-C answers, the examiner's comments point out areas for improvement, specific problems and common errors.

Moving-image text: television advertisement

Candidates were required to provide a text reading of an advertisement for Adidas 'Climacool' trainers, which was 30 seconds long and featured David Beckham, who is associated with both football and fashion.

■ ■ ■

Grade-A answer

The Adidas 'Climacool' trainer advertisement is in the genre of sportswear advertising but more specifically in the subgenre of sports-shoe advertising. It is typical of this genre because it follows the conventional ideology that states 'you are what you wear'. In this advert, the emphasis is placed on the cooling effect of the trainers on those who wear them. For example, there is a woman shown sitting by the side of the swimming pool when, suddenly, wind blows through the soles of her Adidas trainers and then it gets out of the shoes and blows her sunhat off. This example is telling the audience that the lady was hot and that is why she wore a sunhat and sat by the pool. When her hat is blown off her head, she does not give chase, showing a resolution to her problem of being hot, which is only solved through wearing 'Climacool' trainers.

> *e* This paragraph discusses genre and places the advert within a sub-category, identifying some key characteristics. The candidate follows this with a media-language reading of the cooling effect of the trainers and also connects this to narrative theory with some success.

The iconography is also typical of the advertisement's genre and subgenre. This mainly consists of different pairs of the trainers, which in this case are the pairs of 'Climacool' ones. The characters are typical too. The advertisement includes a mixed representation as far as gender and status are concerned. This can be seen in that the first pair of trainers seen are on a woman, then they are seen being worn by a man, David Beckham. Beckham is a well-known celebrity, whereas the woman is an ordinary individual, showing the varied representation of status in the advert. Beckham is used by the institution of Adidas because the company wants to liken itself to Beckham in terms of his style and success. The marketing and promotion that might accompany this advert give Beckham 'star' status. This advert develops that persona fully.

> *e* The candidate continues to comment on generic characteristics and typical features of the advert before discussing and analysing the representation of the product being advertised. The point about the variable image of the trainers (they can be worn by ordinary people as well as iconic stars like Beckham) is well made. The candidate's reference to a number of institutional points about marketing and star status is also good.

The opening shot is in slow motion and it shows a man in a swimming pool. The shot is slow in order to emphasise the need for relaxation and taking things slowly. This is an attempt at value transference, because Adidas associates relaxation with the trainers to attract members of a mass audience who may feel frustrated or overworked. The text offers them an escape from their busy lifestyle.

> *e* The terminology is accurate here and illustrates the point well. The candidate comments confidently and appropriately on the speed of the editing and how this affects the style of the product. The paragraph also makes reference to audiences in terms of their psychological reading of the images in the text. Clear messages and values are being 'given' to the audience in the advertisement and the candidate picks up on these.

This advertisement is set in a tropical area. This was chosen because the cooling effect of the advertised trainers becomes more apparent and is emphasised in a hot area where everyone is looking for a way to resist the heat. All the shots in this advert are bright to show the happiness that there is in this setting, transferring utopian values to aspirational and societally conscious members of the audience. All of the characters in the advert are content with themselves. They are represented as being excited by the new fashion in town (the 'Climacool' trainers) and this is represented by the cool wind that travels throughout the vicinity. This excitement caused by the new fashion represents the characters as materialistic emulators and emulator-achievers who take great interest in brands as a sign of success and status.

> *e* This section is especially strong in its discussion of audience, using correct terminology and applying it to good effect. The candidate uses audience theory to analyse the representation of the figures in the images, and comments appropriately on the use of a tropical *mise-en-scène*.

There is no tight framing in this advert. This connotes that all the characters are free and relaxed, again promoting and transferring utopian values on to the audience. The quick shots that use panning and tracking help to emphasise the speed with which Adidas 'Climacool', represented by the wind, is affecting the area. The primary audience targeted by this advertisement is 12–30-year-old people of both genders. This is indicated through the ages of the characters in the advert, as members of the audience will share common cultural values. The target audience is the social groups of A–C1. This is because people of this class are able to afford the trainers and are familiar with tropical areas they may have been to on holiday. Both sexes are represented in the advert and this will, inevitably, be reflected in the audience. Members of the audience who enjoy football will recognise Beckham and will be attracted to the shoes he wears, so they are also targeted.

> *e* The strongest part of this paragraph is the discussion of camerawork, which, as the candidate rightly points out, is manipulated to associate 'Climacool' trainers with freedom and lack of pressure. The editing is also intelligently analysed, and the discussion of audience definition is supported with textual evidence.

e **Overall, this candidate has understood the text and has shown an ability to use a number of theoretical frameworks to analyse it. Genre, representations and audience are all discussed, though some of the phrasing is slightly awkward. This essay would be awarded a low grade A.**

■ ■ ■

Grade-C answer

The genre of the media text is a sports advert for Adidas. The opening is of a swimming pool and people having fun. The camera zooms in to a lady's feet, showing the image of trendy trainers. The setting, which is a swimming pool in a hotel, then moves on to a street focusing on a pair of designer trainers. Then we see a close-up of a well-known celebrity, David Beckham, a football star posing in a dominant image straight at camera.

e So far, the candidate has not moved beyond description.

The icons you see that are typical of the sports genre are the trainers being promoted and the opening shot of a swimming pool with males and females dressed in swimming costumes.

e The candidate makes the point that trainers are part of the iconography of sports adverts but doesn't develop it. He or she also needs to discuss Beckham and the reasons why he was chosen for this role, for example by giving an analysis of his 'star' persona.

Many angle shots are used throughout the text. This is not to look down on people but to show the trainers that people are wearing. The music is fast and funky and upbeat, which connotes leisure and people having fun.

e The music is characterised but the candidate does not elaborate on its other qualities, such as the lyrics. Pop music is chosen very carefully in advertising and this response needs to reveal more about its genre and lyrics.

The females represented in the advert are young and beautiful, having a lot of confidence and enjoying themselves. The place for the setting, which looks like a swimming pool in a hotel, seems up to date and modern. The males are seen as more dominant and look fashionable. The audience the text is appealing to is 16–25-year-olds who are emulators, and want to have everything they desire. The advert also appeals to young people who are aspirational — they want to be stylish and trendy. The target audience will be from the C2, D and E social groups. These lower-class statuses are included because many of the people featured in the advert are young themselves and want to achieve in life.

e This is a stronger paragraph, using relevant audience theory and synthesising knowledge about media language, representations and audiences to make succinct points.

David Beckham is featured in the advert, and the close-up of him getting into a car tells the audience that he is a well-known professional but you can be like him too. This will make you purchase the trainers. He is seen as a typical role model for the audience to aspire to and admire. I would say that the audience is materialistic and desires everything.

> 🖉 The problem here is that the candidate makes unfounded assumptions, rather than analysing the evidence or considering all the signifiers in the text.

The music spoke out to an audience and created a sense of using your own imagination. It did this through editing the sound, for example there was fast lively music that used quick pauses with the camera focusing upon a close-up on the soles of the stylish trainers which the woman was wearing. Therefore, sending the messages and values through images and making you come to the conclusion that they are saying 'look at me, I am proud of being seen in these cool trainers'.

> 🖉 This paragraph uses poor grammar, switches to the past tense and lacks any application of media theory that might make this a more robust analysis. There is no discussion of how the editing, camera style, *mise-en-scène* or framing emphasise the 'coolness' that the candidate correctly identifies the trainers as expressing. You should analyse connotations, but remember to explain which factors have contributed to your reading.

The people seen in the advert are all pleasure seekers, having fun, looking laid-back, laughing and joking and not letting anything worry them.

> 🖉 The candidate refers to a certain type of character ('pleasure seekers') without explicitly connecting them with a target audience or the product. Always be explicit about the point you are making — the examiner cannot give you credit for implicit meaning.

David Beckham is the key character in the advert and is represented as being trendy and stylish. The audience watching him will want to copy his clothing as he is a successful football player. He is linked to the sports theme.

> 🖉 Again, the candidate does not use textual evidence to support the argument being made and makes a point about Beckham similar to that made earlier. The concepts of non-verbal communication and costume need further exploration. The candidate could also have made use of media studies terminology such as 'celebrity endorsement'.

The adverts create the image that young people should be 'cool' and follow up-to-the-minute fashions and fit in with the crowd.

> 🖉 This paragraph is also lacking analysis of how the image is established. The paragraphs are becoming too short, giving the answer a disjointed quality.

The colours within the text are bright and bubbly, reflecting the personalities of the characters.

The panning shots of the swimming pool could connote being cool, relaxed and casual.

The advert tries to focus on the new trainers to appeal to those who have to have up-to-date clothing. The advert makes the product look desirable by using close-ups of the Adidas product that the characters are wearing.

e Here the candidate comments on some of the aspects of media language, such as panning, close ups and colour, that suggest the appeal of the trainers, but points about editing and *mise-en-scène*, for instance, are neither included nor developed. The short paragraphs demonstrate a lack of development.

The males within the advert are shown to be powerful through clothing and posture, looking straight at the camera, whereas the women are seen as sex symbols and wear fewer clothes than the men. The target audience is therefore made up of males and females as the males can see the characters as role models for being strong and dominant. The females are seen as being beautiful and enjoying themselves.

e This paragraph starts well with some sound points on the representation of gender. However, the candidate fails to see beyond a simplistic reading that men are strong and women are to be looked at. There is no elaboration about how the females may be passive but invite approval from the audience.

The camera moved quickly and outward when the setting changed. I felt that this was done so that the audience could see that we were everywhere.

e Here the candidate would have gained higher marks by linking the speedy movement and editing to a 'youth' style. It would also have been worth developing the idea that the camera has a powerful, omniscient quality and that the audience shares this all-seeing power and feels a sense of control. He or she has also lapsed into the past tense.

The audience will spend a lot of money on fashions and trends because they will feel that they will look cool and be looked up to by their friends. They want to aspire to something as the advert makes the audience relate to Beckham as they want to achieve his success.

e The final paragraph, especially the last sentence, sounds rushed and unstructured.

e **Overall, this candidate uses some of the Key Concepts, such as media language and representation, better than others. From time to time the analysis becomes unfocused, muddled and poorly structured. This essay would achieve an average grade C.**

Printed text: magazine

These essays analyse the front cover, contents pages and editorial section of the May 2003 edition of *Maxim* magazine.

MAXIM editorial

This is what happens when you pay people to tattoo cover stars. Obviously we decided to do it in Arabic and equally obviously we needed a translator. So I rang him up.

You know the Arabic words we're going to 'tattoo' on Tatu? 'Yes, why?' Well, Yulya [the darkish, elf-like one] has actually had one of the words tattooed on her behind already. 'Really?' Yes, really. We're interviewing her now and she wants to know what it means. Thought we better tell her as she's stuck with it for life. 'You mean she's had a tattoo and doesn't know what it means?' Yes… well, we thought you'd written 'love' underneath. 'Did I? What did the word look like?' It's like a capital U, underlined with a squiggle. 'Ah, no. That's "Salaam" — hello.' But you promised love'. 'You can't hurry love.' Er, thanks for the gag, but what shall we tell her? 'To have the other buttock tattooed with "boys"?'

And thus, suitably confused, we set off to interview the two hottest properties in the world of Russian pop. Correction: the only properties in Russian pop. But what property, beautifully appointed and offering breathtaking views. You decide in the shoot the world is waiting to see.

Of course, 'boys' is particularly inappropriate when it comes to the fastest growing, sexually confusing legend that is Tatu. But stick 'our' on the front and it applies to the men of 617 squadron RAF who kindly took us on a mind-blowing, low level spin at 250 feet before heading for the Gulf. Turn to page 112 to read how heart-stoppingly frightening it is to fly a Tornado bomber at 500mph above the North Sea. We can only imagine what it is like over Iraq.

Thanks gentlemen. This issue is for you.

Tom Loxley Editor-in-Chief

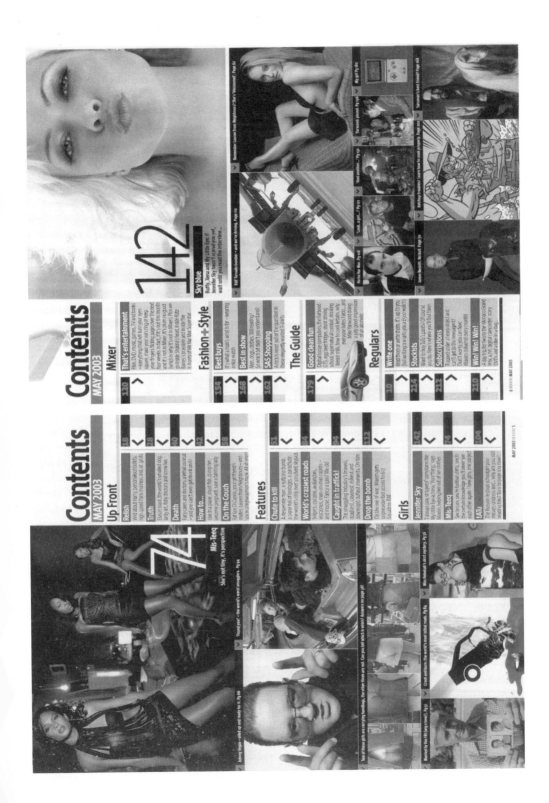

Grade-A answer

The first notable aspect is the banner at the top of the front page, listing a number of key features that are of potential interest to the target audience. The way that it lists them is like an information screen in a train station or on a computer monitor. The fact that there are lots of items makes the magazine look interesting and 'packed', which will reflect the values of the audience members, who believe that their lives are busy too. Many of these articles are represented through small soundbites and this will also appeal to the target audience, which sees itself as having little spare time.

> *e* This is a confident start in which the candidate makes connections between stylistic features and content and then links them to audience. It is immediately apparent that the candidate's analysis is systematic as it starts at the top of the text and works down.

From this contents banner we can make some inferences about the target audience. Females (ironically referred to as 'ladies') feature, along with other things that young men are stereotypically associated with, while the use of black and red gives the banner a devilish quality — perhaps this is a risqué list that gets the audience excited. The audience being targeted is probably males in their late teens to mid-20s, with a disposable income.

> *e* The candidate identifies the use of irony (though without fully analysing how this operates) and evaluates the magazine's colour scheme effectively, linking the demonic feel to the aspirations and consumption tastes of the 'danger-loving' target audience.

This text is clearly constructing a style and look that are laddish and not altogether politically correct. This is signalled through the central image that dominates the front page, which depicts Tatu (a pop duo notorious for their lesbian behaviour on television) in a pose that is both provocative and inviting. The women stare at us, the audience, and look as though they have just been caught in a compromising situation. They have good complexions, youthful faces and innocent expressions, but they wear skimpy underwear which references porn shots and images in adult magazines. One of the women is wearing black knickers with a white top that appears to have been ripped, perhaps playing to male fantasies.

> *e* The candidate makes a thorough analysis of how the audience is being positioned by the text and gives effective descriptions of the probable dominant readings. Typical features of this kind of magazine are identified, including intertextual references, which here takes the form of borrowing styles from other texts. There is strong use of media language, such as colour, typography and layout.

The representation of the women might be argued as being negative, since they are 'caught' by the camera; even in their intimate moments they are at the mercy of the male gaze of the magazine's readership. The alternative to this is to interpret the representation as showing a marginalised group on the front cover of a magazine, without compromising their sexuality.

> The candidate discusses representation maturely and gives two readings from different points of view, which enriches the analysis.

The text treats lesbianism as attractive to male, heterosexual consumers. The women are photographed against a light-blue background, which gives a natural quality to the image, but of course it has been posed for and is thus constructed.

> This paragraph moves subtly into how ideologies are formed and perpetuated by texts such as these.

The masthead is partially covered by the heads of the two women. To some audience members, this might be seen as positive: Tatu are bigger than the magazine and are dominant. Another connotation is that the women are being exploited as their bodies are enlarged.

> Again, the candidate offers two readings here and discusses different segments of the audience. The candidate could have commented that the producers of *Maxim* feel so confident about their brand that they can allow stars to cover the magazine's name, in the knowledge that consumers will still recognise it.

The copy to the left of the main image provides interesting material for analysis. It attracts readers who believe themselves to be rebelling against notions of political correctness. There is evidence of smutty 'schoolboy' humour, directly referenced by the brief 'Schoolboy crush' but also through an intertextual link to *Carry On* movies in the phrase 'Bend over please'. The male audience being constructed here is one whose interests are firearms, danger, 'slobbing' around (evident in the Johnny Vegas brief) and reckless action ('The ten most dangerous roads in the world'). The emphasis on danger, guns and girls is most recognisable through the direct intertextual reference to the James Bond films: 'Tatu — from Russia with lady love?'

> This paragraph makes correct use of print-specific terms such as 'copy' and 'brief'. Genre is dealt with well and intertextual references are discussed fluently. Succinctly outlining the evidence, the candidate evaluates the type of messages that are being connoted and gives a strong summary of likely dominant readings.

The use of language and address is similar to that of a tabloid newspaper. 'THE SHOTS THE WORLD MUST SEE!' is in bold capitals and, although not very big, has the feel of a tabloid style 'exclusive'. The constant use of exclamation marks gives a smutty, brash, 'seaside humour' feel.

> The candidate makes an implicit link to other texts and introduces a valid set of points about how the consumer of this magazine might be likened to a tabloid press consumer and about the type of humour that appeals to such an audience.

Many of these key themes continue through to the contents list, which spans two pages. The subheadings 'Up-front' and 'Girls' are followed by another layer of headings referring to bombs, smugglers, drugs, cars and women. The magazine challenges feminism through many of its images. The dominant image on the contents page is a picture of Mis-Teeq, featuring three passive-looking females with their heads at an inviting angle and their legs splayed from below the knees. The background lighting is low-key and has an uncomfortable feel to it. The emphasis on red and black suggests an underground atmosphere, in which women are available to 'service' men. The women wear revealing tight black dresses that, alongside the single red bulb in the picture, produce connotations of prostitution.

> *e* Some sensitive imagery in the set text is maturely handled here. The candidate comments on the magazine's distinctive style of representation and on the heavy construction of male and female genders in such a way as to please the audience. The intoxicating mixture of 'guns and girls' is highlighted, but the candidate might have discussed how this kind of imagery can be seen as an opportunity for consumers to participate in 'safe danger'. This idea might then have been connected to the 'hypodermic needle' theory of audience reaction.

Maxim's house style continues with the colour scheme used in the contents list as if to re-emphasise the devil-like quality of the risqué representations. The five shots of the girls revealing their underwear and the image of 'Miss Rebekah' clearly signal that *Maxim* sees men as wanting sexually alluring images of women at the heart of the magazine. To some extent, it taps into the feeling that men are restricted in their opportunities to show their 'animal-like' appreciation of women (wolf whistling is now considered unacceptable, for example) and so perhaps they purchase *Maxim* to participate in covertly bad behaviour. Men who consume this magazine want to celebrate the version of masculinity which is suppressed in real life: the lager-drinking, womanising bloke who is invincible, loves gadgets and can even fly a plane.

> *e* This is an excellent paragraph which links generic content to audience consumption through representations and media language. In short, it is a paragraph that meets all the Unit 1 Assessment Objectives.

All of the above points seem to be approved by the editor's page, where Tom Loxley's personal signature justifies the daring and risqué material. The editorial suggests that the issue is chaotic and 'knockabout fun', but all in the interests of bringing the reader the very best. The references to being taken up in an RAF fighterplane confirm the editor's approval for all things laddish and dangerous.

Another point of interest about this page is the institutional detail. Many of the editorial staff (except in the fashion area) are male, which may explain why *Maxim* includes the kinds of features that it does. Most of the female names are in 'Sales' and 'Services', which sets up a parallel between the ideologies, messages and representations contained in the magazine and the gender balance in the positions held by the magazine's personnel. Also worthy of note is that *Maxim*'s international flavour is largely down to the fact that it has so many editors-in-chief spread across the world. This would be a positive thing for an audience to see: it suggests a 'no expense spared' philosophy.

e This paragraph looks clearly at the concept of institution, and makes an important link between the gender balance of the magazine's staff and its patriarchal output.

Overall, *Maxim* successfully constructs an audience that enjoys laddish pursuits and pushing acceptable limits. The magazine creates an unapologetic opportunity for modern men who are forbidden from leering at women in the street to do so through the images it presents. The tongue-in-cheek attitude that intertextually references *Men Behaving Badly*, the *Carry On* films and the *Sun* seems to thrive on the risqué. The magazine positions its audience to think that this is how heterosexual men think and behave in the UK in the early twenty-first century.

e This final paragraph pulls all the strands of the essay together and situates *Maxim* within a set of media texts that contribute to particular ideologies about behaviour in contemporary society.

e **Overall, this essay would achieve an average grade A.**

■ ■ ■

Grade-C answer

There are two women featured on the front page of *Maxim* magazine. They look at the camera and are confident instead of being completely passive. They are, however, half-dressed and this is a negative representation of women. They fully cover most of the whole page and their bodies are perfect with skin that is like a model's. One of the girls has her thumb inside the underwear of the other and this suggests that they might be sexually intimate. This is probably why these two women have been featured on the front of this magazine as the image is connoting that they might be having a sexual relationship and this might appeal to men.

e Many points are raised here but few are dealt with effectively. The candidate should have given a more detailed description of the images (e.g. lighting, colours, composition of the frame, etc.) and then an evaluation of what, when put together, the different parts of the image might signify.

The photograph is a publicity stunt and this will help sell Tatu's album or singles. Tatu fit into the same ideas that *Maxim* do in that they are outrageous, so they share a common goal. In this way, Tatu and *Maxim* are promoting themselves and each other.

e This is potentially a good paragraph, but again a number of issues are highlighted without proper analysis and evaluation. Concepts such as cross-media promotional strategies, touched on in the point about the stars and the magazine sharing the 'same ideas', and a 'common goal', need developing.

There are lots of references to things such as planes, cars and stunts. This implies that the readers are people who are rugged and full of action. Perhaps some readers will buy *Maxim* because it gives them the opportunity to do the things that they can't do normally (e.g. look at women who are virtually undressed).

🅔 The candidate acknowledges the possibility that some men may buy the magazine in order to participate vicariously in pursuits that are otherwise closed to them, but makes this point in a less sophisticated way than the grade-A candidate.

Some of the women are shown in vulnerable positions, as if they have been told that they are posing for men to look at them. The image of Mis-Teeq has been constructed so that they look like strippers. Although the representation of the women is negative, the women look straight at camera and are fully in charge of their sexuality — they know that they are in control.

🅔 The candidate shows an awareness that the image has been constructed and makes a sound point about the resemblance of the image to strippers, but without textual detail to support this. The argument that the members of Mis-Teeq are 'in control' is interesting, but the candidate should have discussed how this might be typical of magazines in this genre. Also, the candidate might have made more links between this image and a potential audience.

Some of the men are made out to be stupid as well and this could be a relief to some of *Maxim*'s readers, who realise that they are not the 'studs' that the magazine tells them they ought to be. The picture and brief that promote the smuggling article on page 5 seem to give a little bit of balance to the dominant image of men as being in control and 'cool'.

🅔 This paragraph introduces a new idea about honesty and self-awareness among *Maxim*'s readers. To make the most of this insight, the candidate might have developed the sense of identification that the text is trying to forge between some of its characters and readers.

All of the images have a tabloid feel because they share the same content and genre style. There is an emphasis on women's bottoms and on items that only become newsworthy because there is a pretty girl involved. Also, the copy at the side of the images sounds like a tabloid: 'Tatu — from Russia with lady love?' It uses alliteration to sound 'catchy' and the main red-top tabloids use this style too. *Maxim* might therefore be attracting the same readers. This target audience might be 15-year-olds to those in their late 20s from groups C1 and C2. They will want to achieve more in their lives and this is suggested through the fast cars and planes etc., which the target audience will want to buy or try to buy.

🅔 This is a strong paragraph in many respects. It uses terminology often and wisely. It applies the Key Concepts and links them together by moving from a point on genre to one on representations, then to media language and audiences. The last Key Concept is most successfully employed, with the accurate use of terms and an element of evaluation.

Overall, the text seems to be making the judgement that all men reflect the magazine. They like nothing better than looking at women, drinking and playing with gadgets and toys. The text presents ideas of what masculinity is and what it is to be macho.

There are a number of magazines like this, the most famous of which is *Loaded*. Both this text and *Loaded* seem to know that what they are doing is 'wrong' but they make a joke of it, as if they are being deliberately provocative and allowing people to do what is normally unacceptable. This is summed up by the way that the editor of *Maxim* makes the whole edition into a joke, and by the fact that the shots of passive, half-dressed women are balanced against images and words that make men look ridiculous.

e The candidate would be given credit for attempting to draw a conclusion, but owing to the restricted range of the essay's textual analysis, there is an impression of claims being made on the basis of the candidate's knowledge or experience, rather than directly stemming from the text itself.

e **Overall, this answer would achieve an average grade C.**

uestion 3

Moving-image text: television fiction

The following two essays are responses to the opening credit sequence and the first 2 minutes of an episode of the hospital drama *Casualty*, which was transmitted on BBC1 on Saturday 27 September 2003.

■ ■ ■

Grade-A answer

The credit sequence opens with a bleached white screen and green crosses that seem to fly through the air. This is the symbol for the ambulance service and the fact that it is spinning suggests that the service is stretched. The number and variety of images that are flashed across the screen connotes just how busy the world of the programme's characters is.

> *e* The candidate begins with a confident analysis, linking media language and the arrangement of signifiers to issues of representation.

Very early on in the sequence the BBC logo is seen. This now appears across all of the corporation's products and has come to represent the brand of the BBC. The BBC is a public service broadcaster with a remit to 'educate, inform and entertain', and so the logo sets up expectations about the upcoming drama. Since BBC programmes try to tackle issues that commercial companies might avoid, we expect this hospital drama to discuss difficult issues without compromise.

> *e* Again, this is a confident paragraph which is not distracted by the narrative or plot events but concentrates on concepts arising from the extract. The discussion — through the Key Concept of institutions — of the role of a public-service broadcaster could have been supplemented by reference to a relevant issue addressed by *Casualty*, for example euthanasia.

From the outset there is the sound of the emergency services siren representing danger and anxiety. This poses the enigmas of 'who has been injured?' and 'what has just happened?', drawing viewers in and making them want to watch further. There follows a set of images that merge into one another and present snapshots of horror, as if in a nightmare. One of the most significant images is of a middle-class house on what looks to be a quiet, nondescript housing estate, with a car on the drive that suddenly blows up. This connotes that drama and action can happen to anyone, however ordinary.

> *e* Narrative theory, particularly Barthes's codes, is applied by the candidate. Media language and the arrangement of the image contribute to evaluations of life-and-

death drama as ignoring class boundaries. The reading of the merging effect is strong too, and there is evidence that the candidate is aware that institutions have to make opening sequences attractive to draw audiences in. For an even stronger analysis, the candidate might have compared other hospital drama title sequences and outlined similarities and differences.

Some other images shown in the sequence are of the accident and emergency teams in action on call-outs. The camera style used here is significant in that it is handheld and suggests that the captured activity is realistic, as if the camera is our eyes. Each of the shots is washed in green and has a very clinical feel to it which suits the drama. Two other significant images are the one of a casualty being brought in on a stretcher, which, again using a handheld camera, seems to capture the drama and tension of a patient's arrival, and the one of a heart massage taking place. This is enclosed in a green cross and is composed in close-up to imply the emotional intensity of the situation (will the patient die?).

> *e* The comparison to documentary-style filming is excellent. It draws on realist practice and the means by which the text signs itself as 'realistic'.

Another important signifier in the opening credit sequence is red liquid spreading slowly across the screen. This is undoubtedly blood and appears in a number of key images throughout the sequence. The blood looks so thin at certain points that it comes across as weak and in danger of running out. Its aimless spilling across the screen sets up a contrast with the hectic activity in the casualty unit.

> *e* These are good points and succinctly argued. The comment on contrast is apt, but the candidate might have added that the blood acts as a prophecy of what is to follow.

As all these images flash across screen, so do the outlines of letters: 'A', 'C', etc. Even though the letters appear random and arbitrary, they eventually come together to form the title, *Casualty*, at the end of the sequence. This represents the chaotic nature of the medical profession and the fact that, in the end, there is narrative resolution and coherence. The implication is that people who work in hospital emergency wards have to be able to cope with a fine line between chaos and order.

> *e* This paragraph is soundly analysed and argued, and its points are well expressed. The comments on the ideological values from the first point are developed fluently. The candidate could, however, have mentioned that there are some signs and symbols in the sequence that are not resolved, just as some of the themes and issues in the programme's narrative are left open, with the intention of reflecting real life.

The opening of the episode is dramatic. Within two seconds, a car has smashed through a shop window. This is a dramatic 'hook', designed to thrill the viewers and keep them in suspense about what happens next. Many enigmas are set up, such as 'where are we?', 'who is this man?', 'what relationship does he have to the older man in the shop?' and so on. The sequence barely lasts 5 seconds, yet there are eight or nine shots as the editing is rapid. This is designed to disorientate the viewer, who has only just entered the dramatic world. The technique is effective and allows the audience to share the chaos that the characters are experiencing. The rapid editing also gives a sense of excitement and anticipation.

> *e* This is an excellent account of how drama is built up through specific visual techniques. The process of disorientation is well described.

The Accident and Emergency department's reception area is seen. The camera here is handheld, in order to reflect the fast pace of activity in a busy hospital. Lots of characters cross the screen in front of the camera as it swings round in a long-duration take to give the impression that a huge amount is going on. The title of the episode is displayed — 'Perks of the job' — and this immediately sets up a paradox: what possible perks can there be in such a stressed environment?

> *e* The candidate makes a strong analysis of the *mise-en-scène* and employs terminology accurately to suggest what the dominant reading is. He or she makes an excellent point about the paradox introduced by the episode's title, but could have developed this by saying that a gratification experienced by some of the more 'informed' sections of the audience would be an enjoyment of irony.

The episode conforms to typical hospital dramas in terms of its generic characteristics. Iconographically, there are signifiers such as green uniforms, ambulances, hospitals with corridors and waiting rooms etc. A typical narrative style of this kind of drama is that many 'threads' are spun at the beginning of the episode. This sequence introduces the victims of the car crash, the doctor who might be leaving Holby City, the issue of stress for the staff, and the question of whether the American woman will sue the ambulance driver for her 'bad driving'.

> *e* The candidate would gain credit for highlighting typical generic features such as icons, narratives, themes and settings. A comparison with other programmes in the same genre would have developed this further.

The episode begins to open up a number of 'hooks' and enigmas. A young man tries to help the woman in the crashed car, but should he be moving her? Will the hospital be able to cope? Will the man's father survive? Back in the hospital we see a senior doctor giving a reference for another doctor, perhaps unwillingly, and ask ourselves 'who is leaving?' The health service is represented as chaotic and disorganised through busy scenes involving extras who criss-cross in front of camera. As an audience, we are positioned so as to sympathise with characters trying to cope with the burden of being overworked.

> *e* The point about how the audience is positioned shows a good understanding of how this kind of text operates.

This is emphasised by the American flight attendant who is seen in the back of an ambulance. She is dissatisfied with the 'service' she is getting and makes it plain that it is very different in America. Her inclusion in the episode raises a number of issues in the narrative and highlights the differences between the American and UK health systems. It is a typical characteristic of hospital dramas to include narrative threads that ask the audience to reflect on, for instance, debates about funding, resourcing and standards of care.

> *e* The candidate raises an interesting ideological issue, thus challenging the theory that audiences are passive when watching pulp dramas such as *Casualty*. The response implies that viewers can enter into topical debates through drama, just as they can by watching documentaries, news or current affairs programmes.

The sequence ends with Comfort, the paramedic who is driving the ambulance, seeing an apparition of a child crossing the road. The dialogue signifies that this refers to a previous episode, suggesting that the series deals with ongoing issues about ambulance personnel and the way that they relive traumatic incidents of this kind. This narrative thread also hints at one of the other qualities of this programme: its similarity to soap opera. Comfort's trauma will be followed through a number of future episodes and this is a device that will keep the audience watching.

> *e* This well-expressed analysis brings out features of content and style such as running themes and the fact that they relate to soap opera structures. The candidate might also have brought in institutions by pointing out that screenwriters use these structures because soap operas are the most successful genre in the UK today.

Overall, this extract of *Casualty* offers a wide-ranging of audiences something to engage with. Those who want topical discussion can enter the debates raised by the text, while those wanting a dramatic storyline are offered something too. The success of the text is due to it being able to be realistic enough for audiences to believe, but also dramatic enough to be entertaining.

> *e* This is a strong response, which uses a range of media terminology and Key Concepts to make an intelligent analysis.

> *e* **Overall, this response would achieve an average grade A.**

■ ■ ■

Grade-C answer

The opening credit sequence of *Casualty* is interesting to analyse. This sequence is seen by millions of viewers each week and has many features that aim to get the audience involved. In the first part of the sequence there are a number of green crosses. These are symbolic of the medical and emergency teams who work in hospitals. The crosses are part of a number of images that appear to move in and out of the screen, almost randomly, but seem to connote that the world that we are about to enter is one that is busy and chaotic.

e This is an effective start and introduces a number of key ideas that will hopefully be developed later. The reading of the iconography connoting a chaotic world is appropriate.

Within the credit sequence there are a number of images that suggest that this is an Accident and Emergency environment. For instance, there are shots of a police motor-cyclist arriving on the scene of what might be an accident. The camera looks as though it is handheld and this gives a feeling of realism. As the images flash past they suggest that the show will be busy with lots going on.

e The programme's relationship with documentary and realism is soundly identified and the reference to the camera supports this. However, there are other scenes in the opening sequence and the candidate could have to referred to these too.

The emergency services seem to be represented positively as they are seen doing jobs that are very difficult and they are under pressure. This is also connoted by the types of shot that are used. There is a lot of red and green and these are typical colours for hospital shows. The green represents the gowns and the red stands for danger. This is a dangerous place to work. The white background has a pure effect, as if the whole NHS was trying to be perfect and the red and the green was covering it and stopping it from doing its job properly.

e The first part of the paragraph is focused, with an analytical point about repre-sentation, which is well supported. Sometimes a lack of familiarity with exam technique makes candidates panic about time, however, and this seems to have happened in the second part of this paragraph, where the comments about colour are not fully explored. The candidate could have given an example from the sequence to support the final point.

The opening of the drama is very exciting. There isn't an establishing shot like there is in most films and TV programmes. This is intentional. It is meant to make the viewers not know where they are. Seconds later a car crashes through the window of what turns out to be a shop. The editing of the sequence is very fast and there are about 10 shots from different angles. This quick editing makes the audience feel excited about the incident. The special effects are excellent too and make the crash look realistic. The timespan of the shots increases immediately after the crash and this gives a slowed-down effect, like many crash victims report experiencing when inter-viewed afterwards.

e Again, this candidate demonstrates good knowledge of film and television concepts and gives a strong analysis of the editing techniques.

We then cut to the hospital. It is another busy day. This is shown by the camera, which doesn't cut at all, almost to continue the suspense. Lots of activity happens in front of the camera, some of which is not explained at this moment. The representations here show that the NHS cannot cope with the amount of work that the doctors and nurses have to do. *Casualty* shows the punishing lives that the characters lead and this is emphasised by occasional close-ups of a character whose expression suggests stress or pain.

> *e* It is a pity that the points raised in the first paragraph of the essay are not linked to the assertion made here. This would have taken the response to a higher level of sophistication.

The text brings up issues that are in the news about the NHS. When the American woman is in the back of the ambulance she says that the American health service is far superior to that in the UK. This allows the audience to take sides and think about whether our system needs reforming. The camera is in the back of the ambulance and we see the American woman whining a lot, so the director may want us to dislike her and the way that she runs the NHS down. There are a few close-up reactions to her. I don't think that the producers want to represent her very well.

> *e* Again, this paragraph could have been developed into a good analysis, especially with regard to the camerawork around the American woman, but some of the points are blunt and unsubstantiated. The candidate's style is too colloquial.

The episode keeps cutting between this story and the car crash at the shop. The way that it does this is a bit like a soap opera. In soap operas, there are different storylines taking place at the same time and you believe that they continue when you are not looking. This is what we believe real life to be like, so *Casualty* connects with its audience very well and is popular (for these and many other reasons, outlined above).

> *e* The comparison to soap operas is a good one and the point about audience in the final sentence shows some insight, but the vague reference to 'other reasons' for the popularity of *Casualty*, 'outlined above', is misleading, since the candidate has included nothing of any substance on audience so far.

The episode is easily recognisable as being a hospital drama. This is because it has visual things like gowns, uniforms, ambulances, blood etc., so that when we turn on we know what it is. There are lots of different stories, which criss cross, and audiences enjoy that — it keeps us in suspense, waiting for the next bit. The setting is a hospital and the locations where accidents happen. We always know that a character who is 'new' and has not been seen before will probably end up in hospital or being involved in the plot. Audiences enjoy the guessing game that this creates. It is called an enigma and is like piecing a jigsaw together.

> *e* Perhaps rather belatedly, the candidate refers to genre and works systematically through iconography, settings etc. The point on interweaving narratives is repeated from the previous paragraph, but is now linked to audience gratification. The paragraph ends with some effective comments on viewers' active participation in the construction of a text.

The audience for *Casualty*, judging by this episode, is of all ages. I think that the BBC aims to get a wide range of people watching. The audience gets enjoyment from the

horror of the images, from following the personal lives of the nurses and doctors, and from getting involved with the issues that the programme brings up. *Casualty* is shown after 8 p.m. on Saturdays and so this means that it is approaching the watershed, which will limit the age of the audience to approximately 12 years or above. Also, the stories do have to be a bit sanitised to avoid offending viewers.

e This discussion of audience might have been more useful towards the beginning of the response. The final point needs clarification and illustration through examples.

e **Overall, the problem with this response is that it is badly organised, as the final paragraph exemplifies. Some potentially excellent points are introduced too late in the response to be developed properly, while some of those mentioned at the beginning of the essay are never returned to and developed. This candidate would be awarded a high grade C.**

Printed text: local newspaper

The following two responses are analyses of the front page of the *Yorkshire Post*, Saturday 4 October 2003 (see page 56).

■ ■ ■

Grade-A answer

The first thing to notice is that the layout of the front page is very 'tidy' and symmetrical. The stories appear in horizontal strips. The overall effect makes the newspaper seem extremely organised and a further connotation of the uncluttered appearance is the notion that the news covered will be fair, balanced and accurate.

> *e* The candidate makes a very confident start with an overview of the page using media terminology. The concept of composition is employed to discuss the connection between layout and readers' expectations.

Starting with the masthead, it seems that clarity is a feature of this newspaper. The title of the text is the *Yorkshire Post* and this is printed in bold capitals which give it importance and stature. There is a large amount of white space on either side of the masthead; this is usually frowned upon in the newspaper trade as an extravagance, so the use of it here suggests that the producers are proud of the masthead and name and want to make them more conspicuous. Also, the lack of an earpiece either side of the masthead may suggest that the producers don't want to clutter the front page or that they don't have a reliance on advertising, promotions and special offers; in either case, they seem to be connoting that the news comes first.

> *e* Correct knowledge of terminology is evident in the use of 'masthead', 'white space' and 'earpiece'. The candidate gives an intelligent reading of the newspaper's unusual use of white space, and the comment on the lack of advertising shows signs of critical autonomy.

Also of interest is the tag-line or slogan that appears above the masthead. Clearly this is seen as an important feature and is given 'top billing'. Yorkshire is a large region in England but, judging from the slogan, the paper sees itself as being at the centre of a much bigger map: it describes itself as Yorkshire's 'National Newspaper', implying that it carries news that has local relevance and yet national importance. This is perhaps a form of 'positive bias' and shows that the editorial board is keen to give a public-relations 'spin' to Yorkshire stories.

> *e* This reading is very shrewd. It takes all the evidence and pieces together a competent and well-explained rationale. There is also an awareness that newspapers are not solely platforms for news reporting but have, to a greater or lesser extent, public-relations functions too.

4

question

YORKSHIRE'S NATIONAL NEWSPAPER

YORKSHIRE POST

50p

SATURDAY OCTOBER 4 2003

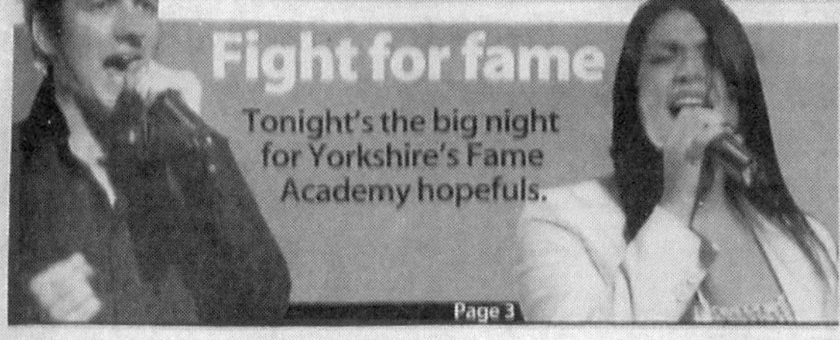

Fight for fame

Tonight's the big night for Yorkshire's Fame Academy hopefuls.

Page 3

THE LAKES IN STYLE FOR ONLY £49. Great reader offer.

Page 10

1,000 people. 100 homes. 4 hours. £12m. The amazing statistics of a property boom.

Page 6. Plus Property in Section C

Disaster fear as toxic ships are cleared to sail

Mike Waites, David Garner and Dave Mark

WASHINGTON of an environmental disaster on the Yorkshire coastline were raised last night as it emerged a fleet of toxic 'ghost ships' are to be dismantled in the North East would be towed along the East Coast.

The ships could set within days after an American judge yesterday gave the go-ahead for the rusting vessels to be towed across the Atlantic from the United States.

British authorities are still to give their approval to the journey that will mean up to 13 ships contaminated with deadly chemicals, asbestos and heavy diesel being hauled through some of the busiest shipping lanes in the world. In the English Channel, and along the East Coast to be broken up at Hartlepool.

Friends of the Earth is trying to mobilise international opposition to the ships' passage, which needs approval from a number of European countries, as part of a last-ditch effort to block the fleet.

One furious MP blamed the Government for letting Britain become a dumping ground for "clapped-out, environmentally dangerous" ships.

The plans have caused controversy in the United States but court action to stop the contaminated US Navy ships

Seabirds at risk: Ken Proud at Bempton Cliffs.

being towed out of Virginia has so far failed.

Campaigners fear one or more of the vessels could break up during the 4,000-mile crossing, causing an "environmental disaster".

A judge in Washington yesterday ruled that four ships could be allowed to leave and another court hearing will be held on October 20 to decide the fate of the other nine.

Able UK, which will dismantle the ships at Hartlepool, has maintained there will be no environmental problems.

Final approval for the journey could be given by the middle of next week once agreement is reached between the British, Irish, French and Belgian maritime authorities over the passage plan. The journey is likely to take at least 25 days.

The Maritime and Coast-

guard Agency has dispatched inspectors to the US to report on the condition of the vessels. They have decided that once remedial work has been carried out the ships will be seaworthy.

MCA spokesman Mark Clark said: "They could pose a risk but once the work is completed they will not represent a threat to the UK shoreline any more than other legitimate shipping came inshore," she said.

But Sue Jolliffe, of Friends of the Earth in Hull, said there were a number of sensitive areas along the East Coast from East Anglia to Yorkshire.

"There are so many river estuaries and wildlife sites – it would be tragic if anything came inshore," she said.

The Royal Society for the Protection of Birds, which looks after vital nesting sites

along the East Coast, said it was "concerned".

Ken Proud, of Bempton Cliffs Nature Reserve, said: "This is the last thing we need. Seabirds are more at risk from pollution than land birds, and it has contributed to the falling numbers of various seabirds."

A spokesman for the RSPB added: "We've been following the situation because of the possible impact along the coast. We are now assessing our position but it is giving us some cause for concern as it does appear to be an issue which could have a potentially harmful effect on wild birds."

A spokesman for environmental pressure group Surfers Against Sewage said: "As well as the imminent danger to the marine environment, water users and residents of the North East, there is further concern that if this activity is given the go-ahead it will set a precedent for similar activities in the future."

But the chairman of Scarborough Inshore Fishermen's Society, Fred Normandale, had "no qualms whatsoever" about the ships being towed through his members' fishing grounds.

"There are too many environmentalists looking for any bandwagon to jump on. Every environmentalist group seems to think they

Continued on Page 5.

Clapped-out: Rusting hulks of the 'Ghost Fleet' anchored on the James River off Fort Eustis, Newport News, Virginia.

Now the victims of crime could be locked up

TOUGH new proposals could see the victims of crime arrested and even jailed if they fail to give evidence in court, it emerged yesterday.

The Home Office said it was considering new measures to force victims and other witnesses to give evidence, to increase convictions.

Asking people to submit their views on whether the proposal should go ahead, Ministers said it would apply to Crown Court trials, and possibly cases in magistrates courts.

The court would be able to issue an arrest warrant if the witness failed to comply with a "witness order" compelling

them to show up at a trial. They could face up to three months in jail for contempt of court.

The measure would be one way to deal with witnesses who were being intimidated by alleged offenders, the Home Office suggested.

Tory Shadow Home Secretary Oliver Letwin immediately attacked the proposals as "utterly unbelievable", while the charity Victim Support said the Home Office's plans "completely ignored" victims' needs.

Existing laws allow courts in England and Wales to issue a "witness summons" if information suggests a witness is

unwilling to attend, and to issue a warrant for arrest.

The courts have to be satisfied that the witness can provide "material evidence".

A Home Office spokeswoman said that under the new proposal there would be no requirement regarding the quality of any evidence the witness may be able to provide.

The court must simply be satisfied that the witness will fail to turn up, she added.

Home Office Minister Baroness Scotland said: "This consultation will enable us to make an informed decision on the proposed reintroduction of a revised witness order.

"These measures are another step in ensuring we put the interests of victims and witnesses at the very heart of the criminal justice system.

"Each time a case is not brought to trial, or a trial collapses, a victim's suffering is made worse and public confidence in the system is undermined.

"We are exploring a wide range of options on how best to ensure more witnesses come to court."

For the Tories, Mr Letwin said: "I simply can't believe this.

"I thought the Home Secretary was telling us that he

wants to make life easier for witnesses and victims.

"Now we have an announcement from his own office which tells us they are thinking of making life tougher. It is utterly unbelievable."

A spokeswoman for Victim Support said: "We have a real problem with this.

"Forcing witnesses to give evidence is completely ignoring their needs and a lot of people find the whole prospect of going to court very intimidating.

"If they get a summons saying they have to be there it is not going to help things at all.

"In fact, it will leave them with a very negative feeling

about the whole criminal justice system."

Witnesses who failed to show up led to more than 30,000 cases being abandoned in 2001, according to Home Office figures.

In 2002-03, about 23 per cent of 55,493 Crown Court trials faltered – a quarter of which was down to witnesses not attending.

Some commentators believed witnesses experiencing "low-level intimidation" about an impending court appearance could find life easier if they were compelled to attend, a Home Office spokeswoman said yesterday.

Strip torn off – then nudist re-arrested

Grace Hammond

A MAN attempting to walk naked from Land's End to John O'Groats was last night behind bars after being re-arrested only hours after walking free from court.

Stephen Gough, 44, also known as the naked rambler, was arrested on the Cromarty Bridge, between the Black Isle and Rosskeen, in Ross-shire, in the Highlands.

Earlier, he had been admonished after being found guilty of a breach of the peace during his trial at Dingwall Sheriff Court.

Northern Constabulary would only say that a man was arrested on the bridge at 3pm.

Gough, 44, was admonished after

appearing in court – where he wore only a blue blanket tied round his waist – after being convicted of conducting himself in a disorderly manner and committing a breach of the peace when he was seen walking naked in woods near Tore in Ross-shire in August.

Gough, of Eastleigh, Hampshire, had represented himself at the trial.

He said he was aiming to prove to society that the naked human form was acceptable.

During the trial, at which he represented himself, he broke down crying and said he was not doing anybody any harm.

Gough said: "Occasionally people have expressed that I am doing harm to children. I do not feel that is the

case." Earlier the court heard evidence from Kathleen MacDonald, 52, who lives near a wooded area in Tore.

She told the court that one day in August she was in her house alone when her two dogs started barking outside.

She told the court: I went outside to see what they were barking at.

"One of the dogs had started running up the road and on the road there was a gentleman with no clothes, just a rucksack and white flag."

Mrs MacDonald said she saw the man, later established to be Gough, walking into the woods.

Mrs MacDonald, who said she "felt quite intimidated" by what she saw,

decided to phone the police. She said: "My concern was that there were a lot of people in the woods, such as people exercising and even young children.

"I felt that if I had been in the woods and I saw him I would have been more than intimidated, I would have been very, very frightened."

Cross-examining Mrs MacDonald, Gough asked her: "What's your belief about public nakedness?"

She replied: "I've absolutely no problem with people choosing to be naked so long as they do not offend the general public.

"I feel that we live in a society that has laid down rules for its and...we should adhere to these rules."

Dressing down: The naked rambler.

Arts/entertainment	13	UK & World News	14
Business Post	15,16	Letters to the Editor	17
Classified	Section D	Regional News	8-9
Comment	17	Money Post	16
Equestrian Post	21-24	Motoring	Section B
Family Notices		Property	Section C
Farm & Country Post	19-20	Sport	25-30
News	2,3,4,5,6,7,10,11	TV and Radio	2 & magazine

If any section of your Yorkshire Post is missing, it is not your newsagent's fault. Please call the helpline on **0800 169 5541** between 9.30am and 3pm and we will send it to you without delay. email missing.supplements@ypn.co.uk

Bright and breezy, feeling chilly.

Full forecast: Back Page

0113 243 2701

Weather / Contact us

In relation to genre, the newspaper has many of the typical features of a regional daily newspaper and, indeed, most national newspapers. The brief has three large areas devoted to promoting stories inside the newspaper. The brief is a narrative device that sets up an enigma code that is designed to draw in the potential reader by illustrating how packed and interesting the newspaper is. The features on offer seem to attract a varied readership. The 'Fight for fame' section draws on the fact that two of the three *Fame Academy* finalists are from the region and it seems to be supporting them. This would attract a younger demographic while the next box is clearly aimed at an older one, with a promotional offer for a break in the Lake District. The words 'Great reader offer...' connote that the *Yorkshire Post* works hard to give its readers a service beyond just being a commercial newspaper. The soothing orange and brown colours used in this box suggest a calm and earthy mood — one that readers will be able to escape to if they take advantage of the offer.

> *e* The candidate identifies the subgenre of the text ('regional daily') and then highlights the generic characteristics. This response discusses narrative issues fluently and then links them to audience needs and gratifications. Control and planning are demonstrated by the fact that, in an earlier paragraph, the candidate described the newspaper as carrying news that has 'local relevance and yet national importance' and now goes on to identify one such story in the *Fame Academy* brief. In terms of audience, the analysis recognises that the features in the paper attempt to attract a wide demographic. The candidate also notes that there is a community slant to the paper in terms of it providing a public service; it is not just a commercial media text.

As well as the masthead and brief, there is the date and the price. The price hints at an audience that is willing to spend a little more to get to the heart of the news. Although 50p isn't much, the target audience is probably a D–B demographic, who are traditionalists and 'stay-at-homers', especially since they are likely to have pride in their region. Judging by some of the stories (which I will come to later), the content defines the audience as being those who probably have a disposable income, are 'settled' and are mostly in their mid-20s and above — possibly a Radio 2-style audience. This can be confirmed by looking at the length and depth of the stories; the tabloid newspaper audience is not targeted.

> *e* This section is effective because the candidate uses the cover price to launch into an analysis of target audience. An appropriate intertextual link is made through the comparison with Radio 2.

The broadsheet appearance gives the newspaper a serious look. The inclusion of primary and secondary stories is usual for a tabloid but here there is a tertiary one too, and they are all lengthy, suggesting that the *Yorkshire Post* is dedicated to bringing as many news items as it can to the front page without compromising depth. The primary story takes up half of the front page, which is a measure of its importance in the view of the newspaper. The copy follows the conventions of journalistic style, with the first paragraph stating the 'who', 'where', 'when' and 'what' of the issue. The 'why' is explored later in the copy column.

> *e* Again, genre is discussed in terms of typical features and through a comparison with tabloid newspapers. The candidate shows recognition of the stylistic characteristics of newspaper writing and demonstrates knowledge of the form and structure of newspaper copy.

A large photo accompanies the headline story. It is clear that the editorial policy on this feature is a negative one. There is a high-angle shot, looking down at the redundant ships and therefore positioning the audience to look unfavourably at the situation. The image contrasts sharply with the picture of Bempton Cliffs, where there is greenery; the size of the ship picture overpowers the cliff image and gives a worrying message. The caption emphasises the negative feel of the photograph through words like 'clapped-out', 'rusting hulks' and 'ghost fleet'.

> *e* The photographs are decoded well here. The analysis is competent and argued effectively.

The headline of the main story is not in a tabloid newspaper style. It lacks alliteration, is set in mostly lower-case letters and appears to give facts simply and precisely, without exaggeration. The representation contained in the headline positions the audience to believe that this copy is serious as it contains the words 'disaster', 'fear' and 'toxic'. The use of this 'masculine' vocabulary, the dominant photo of the shipyard and the representation of mainly male spokespersons results in an arguably patriarchal gender imbalance. A couple of women are quoted and, even though they are in positions of authority, they often appear towards the end of the copy. The only headline that has a tabloid tone is the one about the nudist, but this can be read as an ironic reference to tabloid newspapers.

> *e* One of the strengths of this discussion of language and audience is the candidate's evaluation of the implicit ideology in terms of gender, citing evidence from the picture and the vocabulary.

The secondary and tertiary stories also reflect the editorial policy. The headline 'Now the victims of crime could be locked up' suggests that the newspaper is surprised that this new law could even be considered. Almost a sixth of the whole copy space is given to the Conservative shadow home secretary, Oliver Letwin, who uses phrases such as 'utterly unbelievable', and Victim Support, which is also against the proposal, and comments, 'We have a real problem with this'.

> *e* This is a very strong evaluation of the editorial direction of the newspaper. The candidate could have added that newspapers often have a political bias and that the *Yorkshire Post* seems to be right wing.

The final story is more light-hearted and illustrates a human-interest news value. It relates the region to national events and issues by suggesting that what happened to the naturist hiker could affect walkers in Yorkshire too.

e The candidate shows critical autonomy in assessing why a story about a Scottish event would appear in a Yorkshire newspaper. The theory he or she offers may not actually be correct but the argument is supportable. In terms of institutions, the candidate applies a news value that reveals something about the editorial policy of the newspaper. However, this could have been developed to include other news values.

The only commercial advert on the front page appears at bottom right-hand corner. Again, it is not tabloid in style or advertising mobile phones or other products that would appeal to a tabloid audience. Instead, it is promoting a Yorkshire company, which strengthens the impression of the newspaper's loyalty to the region. The target audience suggested by this advert is homemakers and traditionalists who enjoy minimalism. This is reiterated by the simple font used in both the logo and the copy. The autumnal colours give a soothing and mature feel and suggest that an audience demographic similar to that of the newspaper is being attracted instead of an incongruous one.

e The candidate makes effective use of audience theory in his or her approach to this advert. The response recognises that the style and temperament of the advert are suitable for the newspaper itself (which probably suggests that the company designed the advertisement especially for this newspaper). There is an effective link made between the signifiers of the advert and the audience that it is targeting.

The contents banner across the bottom of the page hints at the newspaper's composition. It includes business and commerce but also serves the rural community through sections on farming and horses. Letters to the editor seem to feature prominently; this is one of the main generic characteristics of local and regional papers, allowing the 'local voice' to be heard. Finally, the statement about sending readers a copy of the newspaper 'without delay' suggests that the *Yorkshire Post* cares about serving its community and, as an institution, is responsible and serious about what it does.

e This final paragraph addresses the bottom of the text and shows that the candidate has covered the information systematically. By identifying different features that appear later in the newspaper, the candidate hints at specific sections that would appeal to niche audiences.

e **Overall, this answer would achieve a high grade A.**

■ ■ ■

Grade-C answer

The genre of this text seems to be a broadsheet newspaper, but it is not strictly this. The masthead, the *Yorkshire Post*, suggests that this is not a national paper but one that serves a particular part of the country, which raises the expectation that the news covered will be local or from a certain area.

e The candidate identifies the text's genre, but might have added something about the typical characteristics of a broadsheet or regional newspaper.

The main story uses a low-key, truthful headline and words like 'disaster' to warn readers about what could happen. The editor has therefore decided to use the news value of negativity to capture the audience's attention. This sort of news story targets an older audience as younger readers will not be so interested. Therefore, the reader-ship is likely be people aged 30 and over, and people who are in steady jobs and have their own homes (which connects to the property section on page 6 of the newspaper). It could also be argued that the newspaper appeals to rural people as there are two main stories concerning the countryside (on wildlife and the nudist rambler).

e The first part of this paragraph is predominantly descriptive and lacks analysis and evaluation. The assertion that the headline is 'truthful' is rather naive — newspapers often present a partial view. Although negativity is identified correctly, the statement that editors use news values is wrong; media studies teachers and students use them to analyse texts. The point about a younger audience not liking serious news stories is a generalisation. However, the second part of the paragraph makes some sound analyses about the link between content and target audience.

The masthead is in very bold type and this makes it stand out. It is surprising that there are no earpieces at either end of the masthead. The newspaper tries to be young and trendy as it includes a story on *Fame Academy* with the excuse that two people from the region are in the final. This story gives it an opportunity to use alliteration in 'Fight for fame'.

e The observation that the masthead stands out because it is in a bold typeface is not analytical. It would be better to discuss *why* it is emboldened, perhaps relating it to connotations of strength and importance and how these reflect the way that the news is reported. The candidate adopts a negative tone to discuss the *Fame Academy* story. A more sophisticated approach might have been to link it to audience theory. Similarly, the candidate spots the alliterative headline but offers no evaluation of it.

The main picture is of some ships that are rusting in a dock. The photo looks grey and murky as if the ships are in a bad place. In the article that accompanies it there are comments from different people, such as Surfers Against Sewage, who say that the ships will cause danger. Friends of the Earth also makes some comments. There are a few words which seem to be most important, like 'tragic' and 'problems'. It is obviously a negative story. Interestingly, this long story is continued on page 5 and so it makes you want to read on. It might be argued that environmentalists would buy this paper as there are stories that concern them.

e The final point is the strongest in this paragraph, recognising that the newspaper may be targeting niche sections of society. The description of the photo is the start of a good point, but the evaluation of the signifiers falls short of connecting the low-key photo and the negative spin the newspaper gives to the story. The analysis of the vocabulary is also underdeveloped.

The list of contents at the bottom of the page tells us more about the audience that the newspaper wants to attract. There are sections on farming and the country, so obviously these kinds of people read the paper. As well as being a local newspaper it wants to give world news, but this is on page 14, so it seems less important. In fact, the letters to the editor come before this and so it seems that this local newspaper thinks more of its readers than it does of world news. There are specialist sections for motoring and property so that readers who are not interested in news can go straight to this part without having to read the boring bits.

e This paragraph has potential, but the use of the word 'obviously' reveals that the candidate is making assumptions about the newspaper's readership. The deduction about world news is good, although an evaluation of the reasons for the newspaper's priorities would have improved it. The point about special interests is sensible and is argued clearly, although not in a sophisticated manner.

There is a website address and this shows that the institution wants to seem as though it 'cares' by allowing people in the community to access news reporting and to write to the newspaper and be 'interactive' with the news.

e Although institutions is not a compulsory Key Concept for Unit 1, it is applied well here in analysing the newspaper's motives for publishing a website address. The candidate would also gain credit for including the notion of interactivity.

The advertisement also seems to be right for a more adult audience. It is for The Yorkshire Sofa Company and cleverly reflects the time of year, autumn, by using brown and gold colours. The style of the living room is one that people might like and so the picture could be aspirational.

e This a good paragraph. By referring to an aspirational image, the candidate demonstrates knowledge and understanding of key terms and highlights how the text is linked to the readership.

The representation of the people of this part of the country is that they are only concerned with the countryside as it concentrates on ramblers and environmental disasters. The people who are quoted in the main story are all from the region and this means that they are able to have their say.

e These points are poorly articulated, and not all of them are valid. The newspaper has a bias towards the countryside and the environment in this particular edition, but there are also features on different topics (e.g. the pull-out section on motoring) so it cannot be assumed that these issues are always its main concern. Not all of the quotations are from people in this region (exceptions include the MP) and the point about people having a voice is clumsily made.

In terms of genre, it is a typical newspaper as it has a headline and the usual features of a front page. The words that it uses are in the style of a broadsheet to make it seem serious (and, of course, its size gives this impression too), but occasionally it will try to attract a younger audience, for example by featuring *Fame Academy* contestants who are young. Also, it seems to want to pull a younger age group in by putting arts and entertainment before the more serious world news, which comes a page after. The name 'Post' is used by a number of newspapers and connotes the idea that the news is delivered to you. It could suggest that this is quite a traditional newspaper by using that name.

e This is a fairly sound conclusion in that it links ideas of attracting audiences to content and style, though it could say more on specific audience segments. The final point about the connotations of 'Post' is interesting, but it seems to have been added as an afterthought instead of being developed in logical stages, which could outline:

- what the word suggests
- how this might fit generic expectations
- what this might tell us about news representations
- what kind of audience might be attracted

e **Overall, this response would achieve an average grade C.**

Aural text: local radio

What follows is an approximate transcript of the 'skeleton' of a transmission by Chiltern FM on Friday 10 October 2003, from 17.57 to 18.03. A real examination would not have such a long extract — it would possibly be half this length — but the extract here provides a wide range of features and allows you to practise analysing radio texts.

Rundown:		Seconds:
• Link	DJ to advert	05
• Advert	BP's Wild Bean Café	30
• Advert	Vodafone	30
• Advert	Beal's of Bedford	40
• Advert	Barclays Bank	30
Competition trailer:	'Secret Sound', sponsored by Baker Bros Jewellers	45
Incue:	*'Next…oh yes! More of today's best variety. 60 minutes of today's best mix'*	
News anchor:	MVO: Menu – football rape allegation	
	– outrage over rail contractor	
	– weather warning	05
Sweeper:	MVO: *'This is Bedford's 96.9…Chiltern FM'.*	05
• Story 1:	Football rape allegation — outcue to taped report	30
• Story 2:	Mum jailed for son's truanting exploits	15
• Story 3:	Contractor pulls out of rail maintenance — includes taped report	30
• Story 4:	Sisters celebrate Prince's Trust nomination for cleaning company — includes taped report	30
Sweeper:	MVO1: *'Chiltern Sport, with Riverside Vauxhall — your premiership team in Bedford'*	05
• Story 1:	Erikson not going to be Chelsea boss — includes taped voice of Erikson	15
• Story 2:	Rugby World Cup report	10
Sweeper:	Anchor: *'First for local news'*	
Bed:	Electronic, hi-energy music; no lyrics	
Outcue:	Anchor: *'Now here's the word on money with* **www.musicradio.com***'*	
Incue:	FVO1:	
• Story 1:	*Company 'fatcats' get bigger rises…*	10
• Story 2:	*Women are now working longer weeks…*	10
• Story 3:	*Random drug tests in the workplace welcomed…*	10
Outcue:	*'With the word on money, I'm Amy Capron…'*	

question

Bed:	Music fades out...
Bed:	Different house music; hi-energy beat
Incue:	MVO1: 'With Bedford's 96.9 Chiltern FM. "Timesaver Travel", with elmsbmw.co.uk... All we know about the car in a car. The new 5 series ...'
'Flying eye' traffic report:	FVO2: '... And a couple of problems to worry about this afternoon...the A6. That accident ongoing at the Bedford southern by-pass has happened between the two Wilstead turnings and we've still got those delays on the southbound carriageway as a result. The B530 Ampthill Road stretch in Kempston...that is looking very congested in both directions at the moment...it's all down to a lorry being stuck on the road entry to the retail park...the lorry is actually stuck on that roundabout...erm...and trying to get into the retail park...but that is causing delays all around and on approaches to that roundabout — it's a very busy stretch anyway, the Ampthill Road stretch of the B350...so again, that is looking very heavy. Naomi Gibson with your Timesaver Travel...'

40

Bed:	House music continues over next two stabs:
Sweeper:	MVO1: '...Stuck in a queue? Call the jam line — Bedford 347222'
Sweeper:	MVO1: '...Bedford's 96.9 Chiltern FM...weather, with B. E. T. I. info; keep your business environmentally friendly...whatever the weather'
Anchor:	'Well it's still quite dull outside...' etc.

■ ■ ■

Grade-A answer

The extract is clearly from a commercial radio station as it starts with a range of adverts. The first, for BP's Wild Bean Café, has a man who sounds approximately mid-20s in age thinking to himself as he pays for his petrol. We are given a privileged viewpoint as we listen to him in turmoil. It is easy for us to recognise that he is walking because there is the sound effect of shoes on tarmac. He cannot resist the products on offer and we enjoy his retail trauma.

> *e* This is a confident start that establishes the genre of radio text and moves straight into the analysis. The candidate indicates that narrative is important, introducing the idea that radio allows a special relationship between the medium and the receiver. Reference is made to the fictional construction of the text in a studio through sound effects.

This opening advert and the ones that follow allow us to identify a number of features. The main protagonist speaks with an RP accent (received pronunciation, a non-regional accent which implies a middle-class educational status and background) and so aligns himself with the potential audience of the radio station, who live in Bedford and the surrounding area. He is well spoken, certainly middle class, and his diction and delivery are clear. There is a definite representation being made here. The kinds of voices that emanate from this station seem to be similar to the man in the advert. They are probably mainly male (there seems to be an imbalance towards male voices in the extract) and in socio-demographic groups D–C1 with a possible audience share of group B. They are likely to be a mixture of emulators and emulator-achievers but will be young people (approximately 20–30 years old) who share similar aspirations and lifestyles to those represented through the station.

> 📝 This connects accent and vocabulary, a specific set of sign systems, to class and to the ways in which radio audiences are attracted. There is a clear recognition that the station has developed a particular 'voice', or sound, and that this is a representational device, which raises certain expectations and influences our judgement. The candidate gives a plausible breakdown of audience composition, showing competent use of terminology and good application of audience theory.

The character voices in the Vodafone advert continue this. They are young (perhaps in their early 20s) and have little money, so they begin by saying that their talk will have to be quick. The deal on the mobile, however, allows them to talk and the friend then begins a laborious recount of his gap year. The FVO used later is also young and adds to the 'hip' tone of the advert. The advert cleverly employs a song from the early 1990s ('Can You Dig It?') and so appeals to the 'trendy twenties' who are indulging in the retro music and the over 30s who aspire to regain their youth. According to Dyer's ideas about entertainment and utopia, the two friends enjoy a sense of being part of a unique community. The audience relates to the situation of the friend who talks too much about his holiday.

> 📝 The candidate skilfully and judiciously links ideas about the voices used and how the programme attracts a young audience and an older one at the same time. It might have been appropriate to add some evaluation about how the target audience of this advert reflects the wider profile of listeners. In terms of messages and values, the candidate indicates that the advert may be representative of the radio station in terms of age, aspiration, 'voice' and trendy approach.

Among all the national campaign adverts is a local one for a department store in Bedford. It begins with the MVO asking: 'How far would you go to be noticed?' This rhetorical device is very subtle in drawing the audience in to the rest of the advert. The voice is local, with a hint of a Midlands accent. The MVO also 'drops' a few letters, pronouncing the word 'head' as ''ead', for example. This colloquial strategy is designed to reach the listener in a more intimate way and, while talking about a local store, uses a local register. The 'bed' music in the advert is an easy-listening track but it has been remixed to feature some drum'n'bass samples. This projects to a wide range of young and older listeners. Interestingly, this also happens in the Barclays advert that follows, in which classical music (Vivaldi's *Four Seasons*) is 'chopped' and 'looped' to give it a wider appeal.

> 📝 The candidate deftly explains that commercial radio attracts a wide demographic through a combination of carefully chosen 'bed' music. Two good examples are used and effectively explained.

The in-house trailer for the 'Secret Sound' competition uses a quick succession of sound effects of screeching car tyres and aeroplanes flying overhead to create a 'busy' sound. This adds to the image that the radio station is trying to present — of being slick and dynamic. The montage of local voices from the audience phone-in demonstrates its appeal and reach. It also gives the station a public service feel; even though it is commercial, it cares for its listeners — so much so that it can afford to give away £25000. The MVO in the trailer is the one used for all the trailers, stabs and sweeps. Radio often uses voices that are familiar to the audience. These voices become the 'friends' of the listeners and help make them feel like members of a community.

> The candidate makes good use of media terminology here. He or she applies Key Concepts such as media language and representation and then links them to wider issues of institution and audience. The comment on recognising the creation of a relationship between the radio station and the audience through the house style is well made. Some competent evaluation is presented clearly.

This trailer and other parts of the station's output given in this extract are sponsored by a range of local companies. This is a very recognisable feature of local commercial radio. The station wants to associate itself with local 'names', creating an image for itself as a responsible and sensible member of the community. This means that it contributes to the local economy and also allows local businesses to unite and provide a strong representation of togetherness. The station is seen to be giving a good service. The sport is sponsored by a Vauxhall dealer and the 'jambuster' section by a BMW garage. The dominant reading of this latter sponsorship tie-up would entail a belief among listeners that they could escape the jams if they purchased a BMW. Another useful 'corporate marriage' is the one for 'B.E.T.I.info', whose 'sweep' is 'Keep your business environmentally friendly...whatever the weather'. Clearly Chiltern FM wants to project itself as a responsible broadcaster and so forms alliances that suggest this.

> In this passage, the candidate avoids analysing the three sponsorship examples individually but instead draws them together impressively to give an overall evaluation. The candidate analyses some of the specifics of the sponsorship sweeps, which are deconstructed to give greater insight into the rationale behind them.

The coverage of news is worthy of note too. There is a tabloid feel to the coverage, which uses soundbites as opposed to in-depth stories. Words are shortened — football becomes 'footie' — and contractions such as 'there's' are employed, suggesting that the station wants its news delivery to be dynamic and upbeat. There is a colloquial tone to the anchor's style as he asks 'Have your kids been at school this afternoon? Let's hope so...' and goes on to describe how one boy 'bunked off' school. With Radio 4 broadcasting news at the same time as this output, Chiltern FM seems to be offering its audience an alternative style that may suit them better. The news does include an item with a serious public interest — the story about a contractor pulling out of rail maintenance — but this is much shorter than the last feature, which is the item about two women starting a local cleaning company. This is almost double the length and reveals much of what the station is about. The news values that are emphasised are human interest and consonance (among others), and the report's inclusion of the voices of these local women makes for a much more community-based item, even though it is not 'hard' news.

> The candidate is careful to ensure that the points on vocabulary never repeat themselves. This paragraph explains how language is used to address listeners in a particular style. The candidate draws strong comparisons between the radio station and tabloid-style coverage, supporting each point with accurate quotations. Again, he/she uses the content of the extract to make evaluations about audience and representation and takes account of institutional issues of news values. The resulting synthesis of the Key Concepts is excellent.

The outcue from the anchor is indicative of the colloquial style, as he states that we, the listeners, are now going to get 'the word' on money matters. The 'bed' for the business feature reveals that the station wants to be thought of as trendy while delivering on a promise of performance, which commits it to giving a certain percentage of coverage to news, factual topics and so on. By using a hi-beat electronic 'club' sound as a background to the serious news it maintains a pacy feel and makes the bulletin exciting. This is a method typical of commercial and pop stations, especially Radio 1's 'Newsbeat'. From the clues in the excerpt, this feature is possibly imported from Independent Radio News (IRN) or another radio station, as there are no local references in it.

> This is competent analysis, employing concepts and terminology correctly. By showing how Chiltern FM marries news and modern music, and then comparing this practice with that of another radio station, the candidate introduces an evaluation of genre.

Overall, the incues, outcues, sweeps, stabs and beds all combine with the voice, pace of the music and the 'speed' of the features offered, to give a sense of a dynamic pop-driven station. But Chiltern FM also projects itself as responsible by celebrating its sponsorship and its involvement in the community. The news reports lack depth but other radio stations provide this service. The main demographic for the station is a young (20–30 year olds), local, upwardly mobile and aspirational audience, judging from the features in the news, business items and the choice of advertisers. This extract is typical of commercial pop stations which have similar conventions and voices, blending a mixture of local people and identities with a more national 'feel', and a sense of having their finger on the pulse.

> In this strong conclusion, the candidate brings together all the strands of discussion and articulates them through the precise use of terminology. Representation is a key issue here and is argued well, incorporating evaluations of points raised earlier in the response. The closing sentence shows poise and critical autonomy.

> **Overall, this response would achieve an average grade A.**

Grade-C answer

The sequence starts off with a number of adverts that are for a variety of products. Adverts are on radio stations that play pop music. Often adverts tell stories that make the audience laugh and this one does. Some of the ads are for local firms, such as the one for Beals of Bedford. Occasionally, adverts on radio are very annoying and can make an audience turn their radios off.

> This is a poor start. It makes a number of mistakes. The first sentence is restricted to unnecessary description — the examiner knows what is in the text — and the second is inaccurate: adverts are not only played on stations that have pop music. The final sentence makes a subjective comment, probably mirroring the candidate's own feelings. The appropriate critical vocabulary is not in evidence and the paragraph lacks the precision that is necessary when analysing this kind of text.

The adverts do give us some clues about who the listeners might be. If we look at segmented audiences, these are made up of people with different ethnicity, professions, gender, ages and so on. From listening to the voices here, this station seems to be representing white people as I don't think there are any Asian or black speakers. All the voices seem to sound very similar and this may hint at the way that there aren't many different types of listener listening to the radio. The people sound as though they come from London and speak quite posh. Lots of radio stations have people on them that sound like this.

> The most conspicuous weakness of this response is its expression. There are some strong arguments here but they are poorly expressed. The candidate tries to employ audience theory and then attempts to analyse the lack of diversity of representation. The point on the bland and generic feel to this station is valid, but the candidate could have developed it into a discussion of popularity, formats and the commercial pressures on radio stations of this type.

The use of the Vodafone advert is very clever. Although the radio station is a local one, by using a national advert it tries to be part of the bigger picture. Also, if adverts like these are being put on, then the people at the radio station must want to attract a younger audience. The appeal might be to listeners who enjoy normal pop music but who want to hear local people involved — they may want them to be people that they know and recognise. They often have phone-ins and there are some listeners who have dialled up and done a competition. This is a good example of audience participation and makes the station look like it cares.

> Although this is badly written, there are some good points made here. A shrewd deduction about the reason for running the national Vodafone campaign leads into a discussion of representation and how the radio station aims to present itself to its audience. The candidate could have developed this into a discussion of the variety of listeners, which may be indicated by the range of features in the extract.

There are a few incues (this is where a link is made into the next bit) and outcues, and these are quite typical on radio as the station doesn't want dead air (which is when everything goes quiet). There are a lot of sounds that overlap here and so there are no gaps. This makes the station sound really busy and manic, like lots of stuff was happening all at once and they are trying to get it to us. When things don't go wrong (like here) it makes the radio station look very good at their jobs and so the listener will think that they are professional and have high standards. Often words like 'best' are used and repeated many times. This gives a reading of the station being confident and offering the audience a lot.

> The candidate knows some radio terminology and attempts to use it, albeit clumsily at times. The analysis of the sound is strong, and could have been further improved through linking it to audience and gratification. It is a pity that the point about language is not extended with more examples and a further discussion of how the words used target particular audiences. Again, the register of the candidate's own language is too colloquial and the style poor; avoid using words such as 'manic' and 'stuff' in exam responses.

The newsreader has a deep voice and this is often the case for these people. He also has quite a jolly sound and doesn't want the news to be boring. The bulletin follows the conventions of news programmes as it begins by listing the news in the order that they think it is important. In some ways, their choice of story sounds a bit like the *Sun*, or another tabloid, as they are focusing on scandal and gossip with the footballer story. There are some news values that are used here to choose which story goes into the programme and this seems to be negative and involve famous or elite people, so it sounds like a tabloid.

> The candidate makes some competent points, but this type of 'concept-spotting' (recognising that news has conventions, recognising tabloid qualities, identifying news values etc.) has little value if the concepts are not used to *analyse* the text. The candidate could have used these observations to argue that, by following conventions, the station is attracting a mainstream audience who may not like to be challenged by 'new' formats. Also lacking is a discussion of audience positioning, which should be centred around issues of representation. The expression and grammar are still poor.

The news story on the truants is good to analyse as it is a suitable story to think about on a drivetime show. Both parents who have been working during the day and their children (who should have been at school) will be listening to the news item. This tells me that the station wants to target a wide range of audience from this news story alone. The story about the two women is 'soft news' and shows that the station wants to attract as many listeners as it can. It shows that the station cares for the public and this is good public relations for them. Some critics say that sometimes commercial stations like this use these items to 'advertise' this cleaning company free of charge. But this kind of story has a news value of human interest and this will keep listeners tuned in as it provides a happy ending for the news.

e The candidate's analysis of the scheduling of the truant story is shrewd, and he or she offers some effective (if unsophisticated) analysis. Higher marks might have been awarded if this was followed by a discussion of another item and its connections with audience profile. This would allow the candidate to strengthen the points made about the audience range of the station.

Although the news is read by a man and the voice-overs in the sweeps and jingles are male, there are two women who are given a short spot to speak. In terms of representation of women that is not a lot. They have about 30 seconds each, so male voices are dominant on this radio station. This could mean that the majority of listeners are male too. One of the women gives a short bulletin on business news and so this shows women to be good at finance. This is a positive representation — and she tells a story about how women in the workplace are giving more. The other woman gives traffic news from a helicopter and this is a more typical role for a woman.

e The last point is left loose and unjustified, but the analysis of gender imbalance is fairly well argued and the candidate develops this point into a connection with possible gender bias in the audience. Further comparisons might have been drawn between these issues and the representation of women in the news stories (e.g. the cleaning women) and the lack of female-orientated sport.

This extract is how all radio sounds. There are adverts that are annoying and they put these in between the latest music from the charts. Most pop stations use the Pepsi Network Chart to entertain their listeners.

e Although Chiltern FM does use the Pepsi Network Chart, there is no evidence of this in the extract, so the candidate is applying irrelevant contextual knowledge. This conclusion fails to provide a strong final paragraph, which should draw together all of the Key Concept areas covered in the essay, and is poorly written.

e **Overall, this essay would achieve an average grade C.**